A SECOND CHANCE

Training
for
Jobs

Sar A. Levitan and Frank Gallo

1988

W.E. UPJOHN INSTITUTE for Employment Research

Library of Congress Cataloging-in-Publication Data

Levitan, Sar A.
   A second chance.

   Includes index.
   1. Occupational training—United States.
   2. Occupational retraining—United States.
   3. Manpower policy—United States.   4. Minorities—
Employment—United States.   5. Work Incentive
Program.   I. Gallo, Frank.   II. Title.
HD5715.2.L48   1988   331.25'92'0973   87-37266
ISBN 0-88099-057-0
ISBN 0-88099-056-2 (pbk.)

Copyright © 1988
by the
W. E. UPJOHN INSTITUTE
FOR EMPLOYMENT RESEARCH

300 South Westnedge Ave.
Kalamazoo, Michigan 49007

ii

The Authors

Sar A. Levitan is research professor of economics and director of the Center for Social Policy Studies at The George Washington University. He has been a consultant to various governmental agencies and has served on labor panels for the Federal Mediation and Conciliation Service and the American Arbitration Association. Included among some 30 books he has authored or coauthored are *Programs in Aid of the Poor for the 1980s; Human Resources and Labor Markets; The Promise of Greatness; More Than Subsistence: Minimum Wages for the Working Poor; Evaluating Federal Social Programs: An Uncertain Art; The T in CETA; Second Thoughts on Work; Working But Poor;* and *What's Happening to the American Family.*

Frank Gallo is a research associate at the Center for Social Policy Studies at The George Washington University.

iii

Acknowledgments

We distributed a draft of this book to officials in the Employment and Training Administration of the Department of Labor, the Congressional Research Service, and many others involved in the administration or evaluation of JTPA both in and out of government. Some reviewed selected sections of the manuscript in the area of their expertise; others took the trouble to vigorously critique the whole volume. Although some remained skeptical about the judgments expressed and others were critical, all helped to improve the final product. The names of some persons who reviewed the manuscript cannot be listed due to agency policies. We are grateful and indebted to the reviewers for their contributions to this study, including the very helpful comments of the anonymous peer reviewer.

Richard Belous (The Conference Board)
Gordon Berlin (The Ford Foundation)
Larry Brown and Mary DeGonia (70001 Training
    and Employment Institute)
A. Lee Bruno (Abt Associates, Inc.)
Veronica Campbell (U.S. Department of Labor, Office
    of Inspector General)
Elizabeth Conway (The George Washington University Center
    for Social Policy Studies)
Norman DeWeaver (Indian and Native American Employment
    and Training Coalition)
Evelyn Ganzglass (National Governors' Association)
Katherine Gillman (U.S. Office of Technology Assessment)
H. Allan Hunt (W.E. Upjohn Institute for Employment Research)
Martin Jensen and Michael Erickson (National Job
    Training Partnership, Inc.)
Lydia Diane Mull (Association of Farmworker Opportunity Programs)
Demetra Nightingale (The Urban Institute)
Marion Pines (Baltimore Neighborhood Progress Administration)
Isaac Shapiro (Center on Budget and Policy Priorities)
Ralph Smith (U.S. Congressional Budget Office)
Andrew Sum (Northeastern University)
Robert Taggart (Remediation and Training Institute)

Jon Weintraub (Office of Representative Pat Williams)
Alan Zuckerman (Opportunities Industrialization Centers
of America, Inc.)
National Alliance of Business
U.S. Congressional Research Service
U.S. Department of Labor, Employment and Training Administration

We were also fortunate to benefit from Annabell Lee's mastery of the computer's mysteries, and her ability to transform scribble into professional looking graphs.

A SECOND CHANCE was prepared under an ongoing grant from the Ford Foundation to The George Washington University's Center for Social Policy Studies. In accordance with the Foundation's practice, responsibiity for the content was left completely to the Center director.

The Authors

Preface

For a quarter century, federally funded employment and training programs have proven their worth in helping the unemployed, unskilled and deficiently educated to compete in the labor market. Job training programs complement a host of federal efforts—including education, housing, food assistance, economic development and income support programs—to ameliorate the lives of the poor.

This book scrutinizes the activities funded under the Job Training Partnership Act, which encompasses a variety of employment and training programs carried over from its predecessor, the Comprehensive Employment and Training Act. Complementary federal social programs are discussed only insofar as they relate to JTPA.

Threatened for a time in the early 1980s, employment and training programs had gained renewed support—but not greater funding—by 1987. Five years after the law's passage, it is timely to examine whether the experience of JTPA supports the congressional decision to overhaul CETA. The answer is an unequivocal maybe. JTPA is a resounding political and public relations success, in marked contrast to the unfairly maligned CETA. Business representatives and conservatives—including President Reagan—who castigated CETA now sing JTPA's praises. Though the president was initially a most reluctant supporter of JTPA, his subsequent endorsement of the law has undermined the efforts of his subordinates and other conservatives who oppose the program.

A careful assessment of JTPA, however, reveals that its performance falls far short of the claims made by administration officials and many program managers. The Labor Department's reported results indicate performance superior to CETA, but the improvement may be illusory. Local administrators and training contractors select a more qualified clientele than CETA served, and are tempted to exaggerate results with impunity because federal and state monitoring of JTPA operations is at best cursory. Moreover, by offering briefer and less intensive training courses, JTPA does too little to improve the saleable labor market skills of enrollees.

Opening with a brief review of past federal training and employment assistance for the poor and unemployed, the authors analyze each major component of JTPA, including year-round programs for adults and youth, summer jobs for youth, assistance for dislocated workers, the Job Crops for severely disadvantaged youth, and training programs for Indians and farmworkers.

vii

Inaugurated by the Kennedy administration, federal job training programs expanded dramatically during the succeeding two decades. Reversing this trend, President Reagan, upon assuming office, gained congressional approval for eliminating CETA's multibillion dollar public jobs program. In 1982, following a protracted debate, Congress enacted the Job Training Partnership Act with sharply reduced appropriations. The law also strictly limited stipends for trainees, and transferred substantial administrative authority from the federal government to states and local business representatives. By 1987, the $3.7 billion appropriation for JTPA was less than a fourth of inflation-adjusted CETA spending during the peak year under President Carter.

While JTPA greatly expanded the administrative authority of states and the business community, Congress clearly expected the federal government to guide and monitor the program. However, except for meager federal appropriations, the Reagan administration treats JTPA as a state responsibility, and the failure of states to fill the leadership vacuum hinders the program's effectiveness. Local programs have increased business involvement in management, but there is no persuasive evidence that employer participation has improved performance. JTPA has made little progress in achieving better coordination with related social programs, dashing exaggerated congressional expectations that efficient interprogram cooperation could compensate for radical budget cuts.

The 620 local training agencies rely primarily upon classroom, on-the-job, and job search training. The limited evidence suggests that JTPA improves the employability of participants. However, pressures caused by the law's strict limitation on providing stipends to trainees, and stress on business rather than client needs, have impaired JTPA's effectiveness. The introduction of performance standards was a positive step, but the Labor Department has inadequately supervised the system and placed too much emphasis on the standards, to the exclusion of other means of improving JTPA. Two-week job search courses, unlikely to effect more than fleeting improvement in the employability of participants, have become increasingly common. The duration of classroom and on-the-job training is even shorter than the abbreviated CETA courses. Legal limitations on stipends and support services reinforce the inclination of local administrators to avoid serving individuals most in need. Finally, in the absence of adequate monitoring, local administrators and training contractors may succumb to the temptation to doctor results to report success.

Reacting to massive layoffs and plant closings in the 1980s, JTPA initiated a program for workers displaced through rapid economic change fostered by foreign economic competition. Federal assistance to dislocated workers is an important advance, but to date the program has been poorly managed. Because of federal and state negligence, dislocated worker projects have spent only two-thirds of the appropriated funds, leaving thousands who could have been helped without assistance. Administrators tend to exclude the least educated and older displaced workers who need help the most. Those who do enroll and require intensive training rarely receive it.

In contrast to other JTPA programs, the Job Corps—a federally-administered residential training program for severely disadvantaged youth—has remained relatively unchanged since JTPA's passage. Despite its high costs of nearly $16,000 per training year, observers across the political spectrum have acknowledged the program's achievements. Efforts are now underway to replicate the Job Corps model, which combines remedial education with vocational training in a nonresidential program to reduce costs.

Two training programs designed specifically for disadvantaged farmworkers and Indians have been particularly neglected under JTPA. Budget cuts and inadequate technical assistance have limited the ability of local projects to address the needs of these severely disadvantaged populations.

The concluding chapter discusses the reforms necessary to make JTPA a more effective program. The two top priorities are increased funding and more vigorous federal leadership. Present appropriations allow assistance to only about one in twenty eligible individuals. The Job Corps' outstanding record is attributable to—and not in spite of—federal administration and a generous but prudent investment. Following the Job Corps' practice, JTPA should emphasize assistance to individuals most in need, providing them with the basic education and quality training they require to compete in the labor market. Improving JTPA's operations does not require altering its administrative structure, and in fact such a realignment would impede necesary reforms. Congress has historically devoted too much attention to the division of administrative responsibility, at the expense of emphasizing and overseeing program quality.

A Second Chance is the first comprehensive assessment of all of JTPA's components. The study draws on the work of various researchers who have examined different facets of the program, published and unpublished U.S. Labor Department and General Accounting Office reports, responses to the authors' questionnaires, and interviews with scores of program managers. The usual lament of researchers about the lack of data has substantial credence in the case of JTPA. Belying its professed dedication to eliminating governmental inefficiency, the Reagan administration drastically reduced the collection of information necessary to evaluate JTPA and thus help local managers improve services to their clients.

CONTENTS

xi

1
A Continued
Federal Commitment

On October 13, 1982 President Reagan signed into law the Job Training Partnership Act to help unskilled and deficiently educated poor individuals to compete in the labor market. The law replaced the much maligned Comprehensive Employment and Training Act (CETA) and continued — albeit with substantially less funding — federal efforts to provide training for the poor which began in 1961. Federally financed training assistance reflects a national consensus that many people fail in or are being failed by the labor market not only in recessions, but even in prosperous times. In mid-1987, during the fifth year of the recovery from the 1981-2 recession, over 7 million Americans were unemployed. This represents the highest level of joblessness in a sustained recovery period since the end of the Great Depression a half century ago.

Those in Need

Thirty-three million people experienced labor market problems at some time during 1985. Some had multiple difficulties: 21 million suffered unemployment, 14 million worked part time because they could not find full-time jobs, and 4 million full-time workers earned less than $6700 — minimum wage earnings for a full year of work. Preliminary 1986 data indicate little change. Of those unemployed at some time during the prior year, 21.4 percent had family incomes below the poverty line. In contrast, the poverty rate for those without any unemployment was 5.4 percent.[1] Even those who work full time year-round are not assured a minimally acceptable living

1

standard, as nearly two million such individuals were impoverished in 1985, up 44 percent from 1979.

The unemployment rate has crept upward over the past two decades, and economic and productivity growth has been sluggish since the 1973 OPEC oil embargo precipitated a major recession. The changing structure of American families has also augmented labor market hardships. While the entrance of more wives into the workforce has clearly benefited some families, increasing numbers of divorces and out-of-wedlock births have had a negative impact on family incomes. Single mothers and households of single persons and unrelated individuals tend to have significantly greater unemployment and poverty problems than two-parent families.

A large proportion of unemployment and low earnings — as much as half or more over a decade-long period — is accounted for by a small proportion of individuals with lengthy unemployment spells or chronically low wages.[2] Deficient educational attainment is ✳ a major factor associated with employment problems. The minimum education necessary to compete in the labor market has greatly increased in this century. However, according to a survey by the U.S. Department of Education, nearly 13 percent of adults in this country are functionally illiterate.[3] In 1984, adults with less than a high school education experienced over four times as much unemployment as those with four or more years of college, and the latter earned 2.5 times as much as the less educated group.[4]

Economic difficulties are also particularly concentrated among minorities, youth, and women who maintain families. The incidence of black unemployment and poverty is more than twice that of the rest of the population. While not quite as bleak, Hispanic unemployment and poverty also far exceed that of the total population.

Of all age groups, youth are most vulnerable to unemployment. The level of teenage joblessness is about three times that of adults, and that of the 20-24 age group is 75 percent higher. Black youth joblessness is especially severe: only four of ten black teenagers are in the workforce, and of the remainder two of five are unemployed.

Unemployment in female-headed families is 70 percent higher than in married couple families, and the poverty rate is five times higher. More than half of the black and Hispanic women who maintain their families are poor. Almost one of every six families, and more than two of five black families, are headed by women.

The foregoing groups have traditionally experienced employment problems, but in recent years the problems of dislocated workers have also gained increasing attention. Increased foreign competition and a severe recession during the early 1980s eliminated large numbers of jobs in the goods-producing sector, especially in manufacturing. It is difficult to determine the exact causes of dislocation, but its unemployment impact is not in doubt. Between 1981 and 1985, 10.8 million workers 20 years old and over lost their jobs due to layoffs from which they had not been recalled or to plant closings. A Bureau of Labor Statistics analysis of displaced workers who had three or more years job tenure found that only two-thirds were reemployed in January 1986. Eighteen percent were unemployed, and the remaining 15 percent had dropped out of the labor force. As in the case of other jobless workers, the unskilled and deficiently educated displaced workers tended to fare worst.[5]

The number of persons in need of job-related assistance represents a substantial proportion of the working age population. The following figures are not additive because of overlapping categories, but provide an idea of the dimensions of the problem:[6]

Characteristics	Number (millions)
Total poor (16-64 years old)	17.8
Blacks (16-64)	4.4
Hispanics (16-64)	2.7
15-24 year olds	6.6
Single mothers (15-64)	3.3
High school dropouts (25-64)	23.6
Dislocated workers (20-64)	3.1

✹ Each of these groups may require different strategies to improve their employability. Young people, who tend to have little labor market experience, may benefit from learning basic job search skills. Disadvantaged youth without adequate skills can profit from programs providing high school equivalency or vocational training. The discrimination often faced by minorities may be overcome by partially subsidizing employers for on-the-job training costs and by government enforcement of equal opportunity laws. Women who maintain families frequently require child care assistance to successfully complete a training course. Displaced and older workers usually possess substantial work experience, and may only need job placement assistance. However, displaced employees who have worked for years in a now obsolete occupation may need to be retrained for an entirely new career.

The Expanding Federal Role

Although the federal government has promoted the welfare of the citizenry since the earliest years of the republic, sustained employment and training efforts focused on the disadvantaged emerged only a quarter century ago. Starting with a modest appropriation of $10 million under the Area Redevelopment Act of 1961, annual appropriations increased a thousandfold within two decades before declining during the 1980s (figure 1.1).[7]

Figure 1.1
Federal employment and training financing and services have fluctuated drastically over the past two decades (1986 dollars).

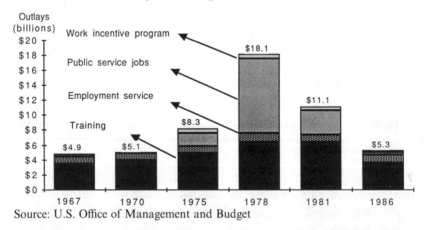

Source: U.S. Office of Management and Budget

Persistent unemployment in the early 1960s resulted in the enactment of the Manpower Development and Training Act of

1962, the first major expansion of federal training efforts. MDTA initially provided retraining for experienced workers dislocated by automation, but was later redirected toward the poor.

In 1963, congressional attention turned toward youth as the first baby boomers reached age 16 and began entering the labor force. Congress expanded support for a federal vocational education program that dated back to 1917.

The Great Society

In 1964 the nation's attention focused on the plight of the poor in response to President Lyndon Johnson's declared "war on poverty." Economists were predicting that projected federal budget surpluses would impede economic growth. What better way to spend the surpluses than to help build a better society? As part of its antipoverty efforts, the 1964 Economic Opportunity Act created two new youth employment programs: the Job Corps, a residential training program; and the Neighborhood Youth Corps, providing work experience. Work experience was also used to help needy adults, including public assistance recipients. Adopting the notion that the wearer, not the cobbler, knows where the shoe pinches, the legislation favored "maximum feasible participation" of the poor in setting program policy. The institutional result was the emergence of community action agencies and community-based organizations as advocates for the poor and deliverers of services, including employment and training assistance.

Meanwhile, the unemployment rate remained stuck between 5 and 6 percent throughout 1963 and the first half of 1964 — a rate considered high at that time. Post World War II economic textbooks had preached that a tax cut — without an offsetting reduction in government expenditures — would help reduce unemployment by stimulating demand for the purchase of goods and services. In 1964, Congress tested this theory, cutting federal personal and corporate income taxes by approximately $14 billion while moderately increasing expenditures. The action was strikingly successful. Unemployment declined to 5 percent by the end of the year, and further dropped to 4.5 percent by the summer of 1965 on the heels of a $5 billion excise tax cut, when deficit spending to finance the Vietnam War took over as the engine for job creation.

By 1965, America's reemergent social conscience addressed the needs of the physically and mentally handicapped, millions of whom were unable to effectively compete in the labor market. The federal government had previously enacted a comprehensive rehabilitation program for World War II and Korean War veterans; new legislation expanded federal vocational rehabilitation efforts for other disabled persons.

In 1966, Congress experimented with small public jobs programs for adults not on welfare, the first such efforts since the Great Depression. New Careers trained the poor and undereducated for paraprofessional jobs, and Operation Mainstream employed older rural residents at conservation tasks. New Careers failed partly because the training required a long-term commitment and because of resistance by professionals protective of their jobs and status. Operation Mainstream limped along with limited funding until it mushroomed into a more comprehensive, multibillion dollar public service employment program five years later. Also in 1966, the Adult Education Act initiated federal educational assistance for high school dropouts and illiterate adults.

Attention turned in 1967 to welfare recipients. Despite strong economic growth since the early 1960s, Aid to Families with Dependent Children program recipients had almost doubled since the beginning of the decade. The cry was raised that if the program continued to grow at this rate, we would all be driven into the poorhouse. Congress responded with the Work Incentive Program, called WIN for short (the acronym WIP was shunned). Work experience and supportive services would enable welfare recipients to secure jobs, economic independence and — as some members of Congress hoped — "get 'em off our backs."

Government efforts notwithstanding, unemployment in many inner cities remained a serious problem. Dozens of riots broke out in the mid-1960s, from Watts to Detroit to the nation's capital. One result was the Concentrated Employment Program of 1967, which put antipoverty and training funds in the hands of mayors, county officials, and community-based organizations to boost job opportunities in poor neighborhoods.

Until 1968, the Great Society's employment and training initiatives had been designed almost entirely by federal agencies. With rising social unrest, the private sector began to pay increasing attention to inner city conditions. President Johnson, seizing upon this concern, created the National Alliance of Businessmen — the "men" was later dropped — to encourage employers to accept direct responsibility for combating discrimination and poverty.

However, by the last year of the Johnson administration, the political pressure to ameliorate the lot the of poor had crested. Economic growth and new government initiatives helped reduce poverty substantially in the 1960s, but dreams of total victory had proven illusory.

Nixon and the Comprehensive Employment and Training Act

The Nixon administration came to power with only one positive commitment in the employment and training field: to consolidate and at the same time decentralize the diverse programs which had emerged during the 1960s. Congress was prepared to accept this approach only if it was accompanied by a public sector job creation program. The administration, however, strongly opposed what it considered "make work" jobs.

The recession of 1970-1 and the approaching presidential elections generated sufficient political pressure to induce President Nixon to sign the 1971 Emergency Employment Act authorizing a public employment program. A $2.25 billion appropriation allowed state and local governments and nonprofit organizations to hire some 150,000 unemployed persons.

Nixon's support of public employment was short-lived. Following his 1972 landslide reelection, Nixon attempted to dismantle the Great Society. Watergate intervened, however, and amid a period of disarray in the executive branch the Labor Department negotiated directly with Congress to create the Comprehensive Employment and Training Act (CETA). Enacted in December 1973, the CETA compromise called for locally-managed but federally-funded training and public sector job creation programs. After years of debate over the appropriate scope and locus of service delivery, Congress gave local governments broad discretion to tailor job training programs to community needs. CETA also authorized a standby public service employment program, to be implemented whenever national and local unemployment rates rose too high. Although most programs were to be managed at the local or state level, the federal government continued to operate the Job Corps for youth and programs for Indians and farmworkers.

CETA began under the least propitious circumstances, arriving simultaneously with the OPEC oil embargo which quadrupled crude oil prices and induced a recession. The new employment and training program was overwhelmed by unemployment, which climbed from a 5 percent rate at the beginning of 1974 to over 7 percent by December. President Gerald Ford reluctantly agreed to a new public service employment program, shifting CETA's focus toward job creation rather than training. Unemployment peaked at 9 percent in the spring of 1975 and averaged 7.7 percent in the 1976 election year. Ford acquiesced to a congressional extension of the public service employment program shortly before the election, but vetoed Democratic efforts to further increase funds for job creation.

A Major Expansion Under Carter

In 1977, the executive reins returned to the Democrats, who after eight years out of power vigorously promoted new employment and training initiatives. The Youth Employment and Demonstration Projects Act of 1977 (YEDPA), expanded funding for public service jobs, and employment tax credits were quickly enacted. Together these programs constituted a major if short-lived commitment of resources to combat unemployment.

The New Jobs Tax Credit of 1977 offered employers incentives for expanding their workforce. In its brief two-year lifespan, over $4 billion in tax expenditures boosted overall employment. The program was not restricted to the disadvantaged.

The highest priority, however, was to ameliorate unemployment among poor youths. YEDPA was a combination of traditional work experience and skill training programs with experimental research projects. Another innovation directed primarily toward youths was the Targeted Jobs Tax Credit of 1978 (TJTC). Similar to the expiring New Jobs Tax Credit, TJTC offered employers a substantial tax credit for employing poor youths and other impoverished individuals.

Another major employment initiative of the Carter administration was an expansion of public service employment under CETA from 300,000 to 750,000 job slots in nine months. The pressure to quickly fill these jobs resulted in isolated, though highly publicized, cases of careless management and enrollment of ineligible applicants that were to haunt CETA for the rest of its limited life.

The last major employment and training development during the Carter administration was a 1978 revision of CETA. Amendments reduced the discretionary authority of state and local governments, confined eligibility for public service employment to the poor, and initiated a new training program which involved private sector representatives in program planning and implementation. The changes improved the operations of CETA and addressed concerns of financial mismanagement, but did little to boost the program's image.

The Job Training Partnership Act

In a clear break with past federal policy, President Reagan mounted a concerted effort to sharply cut employment and training spending along with other antipoverty programs. CETA public service jobs were eliminated in 1981 with little dissent, as exaggerated and highly publicized abuses had undermined the program's support. Negative images of public employment as "make-work, dead-end" jobs had triumphed. Reagan administration appointees ignored evidence that supported the program, and confidently predicted that the private sector would reabsorb displaced public service employees. However, later studies showed that these individuals experienced severe reemployment problems.[8]

CETA's scheduled September 1982 expiration prompted a lengthy debate over the act's remaining job training sections.[9] By early 1982, three major proposals emerged. House Democrats favored a program similar to CETA, but with increased business involvement. The Reagan administration favored terminating the program and shifting the responsibility to states and localities. As an interim step, however, the administration supported a block grant arrangement with federal financing but state control over program operations. The Senate Republicans' compromise solution favored continued federal oversight with a substantial delegation of authority to states and business officials.

As the recession deepened and unemployment rose, Congress balked at the administration's proposal to end federal support of job training assistance. The debate then shifted to the design of a new program, centering on four contentious issues: how much should be spent; whether enrollees should be given cash assistance as well as training; the proper division of authority among federal, state and local government; and the degree of business involvement.

Although the jobless rate was approaching 9 percent, President Reagan's budget, introduced in January 1982, recommended $2.4 billion for job training, only a fourth of the amount appropriated prior to his election. Senators Dan Quayle and Edward Kennedy proposed a bipartisan bill carrying a price tag of $3.8 billion. Representative Augustus Hawkins offered a $5.4 billion proposal, but a cost conscious House reserved only $3 billion for job training. In the final legislation, Congress evaded the funding issue by allocating "such sums as may be necessary" for JTPA. The only exception was the widely praised Job Corps program, budgeted at $618 million for fiscal 1983. Subsequently, Congress appropriated $3.7 billion for JTPA's first full year.

The House Democratic bill initially proposed reviving public service employment. Because of adamant administration opposition, the Democrats decided to strike the job creation proposal to facilitate passage of the training bill. Once this concession was made the issue of income support payments to trainees became paramount. The Democrats considered stipends to trainees and other support services, such as child care for mothers with young children, essential to sustain trainees with little or no outside income. But the administration countered that by devoting over half of its training budget to cash payments and support services, CETA became a disguised welfare program, and the president insisted on limiting outlays exclusively to training and administrative expenditures. The bitter controversy peaked when the House threatened to enact a simple extension of CETA if the administration refused to compromise. Faced with nearly 10 percent unemployment and congressional elections a month away, the administration relented. The compromise required that local job training sponsors spend at least 70 percent of their allocation for training. No more than 15 percent could be devoted to administration. A limit of 30 percent was applied to support services and administration combined. The limitations could be waived if a locality suffered high unemployment, faced unusually high child care or transportation costs, or offered lengthy training courses.

The appropriate division of responsibility between federal, state and local government has been debated since the federal government first enacted job training legislation. Under the initial CETA legislation, local elected officials were largely responsible for program administration. Rising unemployment and program abuses — greatly exaggerated by the media — stimulated greater federal intervention, but by the early 1980s the administration sought to eliminate federal responsibility entirely, prompting an ideological debate between advocates of sustained federal involvement and those who favored a passive federal role. The administration and Senate Republicans proposed to delegate most of the federal government's administrative authority to state governors. House Democrats favored continuing the CETA model, which divided administrative responsibility between federal and local authorities. Although the state role under CETA was minor, inexperience was not necessarily a drawback because governors were not stigmatized by CETA's widely publicized abuses. The National Governors' Association lobbied hard for expanded state responsibility. In response the local governments which had administered CETA — represented by the National Association of Counties, the U.S. Conference of Mayors, and the National League of Cities — argued that President Reagan's federalist principles should naturally cause him to favor administration by the government closest to the people. Out of this struggle emerged a somewhat ambiguous compromise which ensured that the question of program authority would not be settled until JTPA got underway. Although significant responsibilities were retained at the federal level, the law delegated most oversight duties to state governors. To facilitate state authority, 22 percent of the funds for JTPA's largest training program and all dislocated worker financing were allocated directly to the governors. Decisions on who should be served and how to serve them were left to local administrators, within the limits of the law.

Another thorny administrative issue concerned the role of business representatives. Apart from offering on-the-job training, business was hardly involved in federal employment and training programs until CETA's 1978 reauthorization created a Private Sector Initiative Program (PSIP) and established private industry councils (PICs) to advise local programs. Job placement rates were higher under PSIP than CETA programs administered by local governments, probably because PSIP served a more qualified clientele. However, the National Alliance of Business and the U.S. Chamber of Commerce argued that the PSIP experience proved the importance of business leadership in building a successful job training program. The idea found ready acceptance in an administration which fervently believed that business was inherently more efficient than the government. However, the claims made on behalf of business involvement were not universally shared. Arguing that employers were primarily interested in maximizing profits and largely disinterested in hiring the poor, opponents contended that the potential benefits of business involvement were greatly exaggerated. Expanded business authority was also contested by the various interest groups representing local elected officials.

Each of the three major job training bills offered as a substitute for CETA in 1982 envisioned an enlarged employer role. However, the administration and Senate proposals went much further than the House Democratic bill, which would have largely retained the authority of local elected officials. The final JTPA compromise gave business greatly increased power at the local level, but attempted to ensure that employer representatives and elected officials would be equal partners in designing and administering local programs. The PICs were transformed from an advisory to a policymaking council with a required majority of business representatives. Local training plans had to be jointly approved by the PICs and local elected officials, with disputes resolved by the governor.

Despite the general emphasis on reduced spending, the addition of a new program for retraining dislocated workers was not controversial. The problem of dislocated workers was viewed as increasingly acute during the early 1980s because of increased foreign economic competition, the continued relative decline in manufacturing employment, and the deepening recession. Although many dislocated workers had previously possessed good jobs, the difficulty they experienced in regaining employment was thought to justify federal intervention.

Several other new features in JTPA were also added with relatively little controversy. The most important of these concerned performance standards, or numerical criteria used to assess local program success by gauging job placement rates, participants' earnings and training costs, among other factors. Performance standards had evolved under CETA, but JTPA instituted mandatory national targets. The law established monetary awards for successful programs and sanctions against localities which performed poorly.

Congress also supported increased coordination between job training and related social programs. This objective was not new, but it did receive increased attention during the 1982 debate. JTPA incorporated amendments promoting coordination between JTPA and public employment offices and welfare programs. The law vested principal responsibility for coordination with the governor's office and allocated funds directly to governors for coordination activities under JTPA's principal training program.

Congress adopted two other significant administrative provisions designed to avoid problems which had plagued CETA. JTPA was authorized as a permanent program to eliminate wrenching quadrennial reauthorization debates. Second, to provide localities with adequate lead time to plan the coming year's expenditures, JTPA's operating year was scheduled to begin in the July following the start of the federal government's fiscal year in October. For example, JTPA program year 1988 begins July 1, 1988 and ends June 30, 1989; the federal fiscal year 1988 begins on October 1, 1987.* CETA local planners often were not informed of their allocation until the fiscal year was underway because Congress made belated decisions on appropriations.

Although JTPA's passage was marked by extended and heated debate, the political and economic climate during 1982 made it

---

*Following JTPA's practice, references to years in this study denote program years.

reasonably certain that a federal job training program would be enacted. Rising unemployment and the approaching 1982 mid-term election placed enormous pressure on the nation's leaders. From a trough of 7 percent in mid-1981, the unemployment rate exceeded 10 percent by the fall of 1982. Once Congress approved JTPA, President Reagan's initial opposition to continued federal support of training did not prevent him from claiming credit for a program he had long opposed.

Like CETA, JTPA encompasses a number of separate programs. The centerpiece of the law is Title II, which provides training grants to states, a summer jobs program for youth, and set-aside funds for education and older worker programs. Title III addresses the needs of workers dislocated due to foreign competition or technological change. Title IV continues a variety of CETA programs whose administration remains the direct responsibility of the federal government. These include the Job Corps as well as programs designed for migrant and seasonal farmworkers, Indians, and veterans (table 1.1).

Table 1.1
JTPA Program Components

Program	1987 appropriation (millions)
Total	$3,656
Title IIA Adult and youth programs	1,840
State education coordination and grants	147
Training programs for older individuals	55
Title IIB Summer youth programs (1988)	750
Title III Dislocated worker programs	200
Title IV Federally administered programs	866
Job Corps	656
Native American programs	62
Migrant and seasonal farmworker programs	60
Veterans' employment programs	10
Technical assistance, research, and pilot projects	79

Source: Congressional appropriations

JTPA's character was more strongly influenced by the political and economic climate of the early 1980s than by drawing on the experience of two decades of federal employment and training programs. Studies of CETA demonstrated that the program was generally a success and not a debacle.[10] Rather than reforming CETA, however, Congress chose to overhaul the system. Most of JTPA's new elements — state and business leadership, the prohibition of public service jobs, and radically reduced income support payments — were inspired more by faith than evidence. The heart of the program, the type of training which enrollees receive, was virtually ignored during the legislative debate. Whatever the merits of the law that emerged, the torch was passed to the new public-private partnership.

2

The Reluctant Partners
Program Management

As its title connotes, the Job Training Partnership Act is designed to create a working partnership among the three levels of government and the private sector. This approach is embodied in Title II programs, constituting about three-fourths of JTPA expenditures. The law provides different administrative arrangements for the dislocated worker program and, following CETA's practice, retains federal responsibility for directing the Job Corps and programs serving farmworkers, Indians and veterans.

Federal Administration

In comparison with earlier employment and training programs, the federal role in JTPA is circumscribed: principal administrative responsibility rests with the states. Nevertheless, despite Reagan administration efforts to completely turn over job training programs to the states and the business community, Congress clearly assigned the federal government a major role in JTPA. The primary federal responsibilities include financing, monitoring state and local compliance with the law, supplying technical assistance, assessing the program, and ensuring fiscal accountability.

JTPA was implemented under circumstances strikingly different from CETA. CETA had barely begun when it was faced with a major recession, while JTPA's implementation largely coincided with a lengthy economic recovery. Congress altered CETA extensively during its early years, most notably by adding a major job creation program, while Congress did not amend JTPA until four

17

years after its enactment — and then only in a minor fashion. Federal JTPA administrators have promulgated few rules, in contrast to the numerous regulations affecting CETA operations which reflected multiple and often transitory goals. As House Education and Labor Committee Chairman Augustus Hawkins, one of JTPA's principal architects, noted, "The federal government put the money on a stump and ran away."[1]

Virtually all observers of JTPA agree that the Labor Department abjured leadership of the program. The department itself would not quarrel with this assessment, but regards its "hands-off" policy as a virtue. Since the Reagan administration believes that the intrusion of the federal government is counterproductive, limiting federal authority is a deliberately pursued end. This rigid ideological posture has demonstrably hampered program efficiency.

Misguided personnel actions compounded the department's policy of distancing itself from the administration of JTPA. When the program began operations in October 1983, the staff of the Labor Department's Employment and Training Administration consisted of 2000 persons, down from over 3300 in 1981. By mid-1984, the agency had only 1700 positions, 300 below the level authorized by Congress. The staff directly involved in JTPA operations declined from 1000 at the end of 1983 to 700 in 1987. Although Congress has periodically established higher limits on staff levels, insufficient oversight allowed the Labor Department to evade congressional strictures.

Serious congressional concerns about staff cutbacks prompted a U.S. General Accounting Office investigation which found that the reductions adversely affected departmental morale and efficiency. Lost expertise left ETA in a poor position to manage JTPA. Repeated reorganizations resulted in over 200 demotions, and when staff exercised their seniority rights, unqualified persons frequently ended up in technical positions. For example, the head of an ETA administrative office noted that about 80 percent of the staff members in one office had no prior training or experience for their jobs.[2]

JTPA's lackluster leadership was largely attributable to the Reagan administration's first Secretary of Labor, Raymond Donovan, and his Assistant Secretary for Employment and Training,

Albert Angrisani. Donovan's four-year tenure was marred by allegations of improper conduct prior to his assumption of office, although he was later cleared of the charges. Donovan retained little influence in his last two years after then-White House chief-of-staff James Baker publicly advocated his resignation in early 1983. Federal oversight of JTPA improved somewhat when Labor Secretary William Brock and Assistant Secretary Roger Semerad assumed office in 1985. As an indication of their efforts, the Labor Department's 1987 budget request proposed doubling research and pilot project funding (Congress approved most of the request). The department also initiated steps to enhance policy guidance and the quality of JTPA evaluations.

However, federal technical assistance, data collection and research, and monitoring of states and localities remain inadequate. The Labor Department continues to treat JTPA as a block grant program, neglecting its responsibilities under the act. Compliance reviews designed to monitor state and local conformity with JTPA provisions and regulations are superficial, focusing only on technical compliance with the law.[3]

Financing Job Training

JTPA is a much more modest program than CETA. Adjusting for inflation, JTPA's 1987 budget is only a third of CETA's $8.1 billion 1980 appropriation. Even excluding CETA public service employment, the JTPA appropriation is only half as large as CETA in real terms. Budget cuts in the early Reagan years hit employment and training programs harder than any other social program. JTPA funding declined by another 15 percent in real terms during it's first three years, primarily due to cuts in the summer youth jobs and dislocated worker programs and the initial impact of the Gramm-Rudman-Hollings Deficit Reduction Act of 1985 (table 2.1). However, Congress increased JTPA's 1987 budget by nearly $350 million. Over the entire 1983-1987 period, inflation-adjusted JTPA funding has dropped by about 7 percent. The inability of the JTPA community to develop an efficient lobbying network is one reason behind inadequate funding. For example, only one of 650 witnesses before the relevant congressional appropriations committees advocated increases in JTPA funding. The administration proposed to

Table 2.1

JTPA appropriations have declined by 7 percent in constant dollars since the start of the program (millions).

Program	Oct. 1983-June 1984	1984	1985	1986	1987	1988 (President's proposal)
TOTAL (current dollars)	$2893.9	$3732.0	$3643.6	$3311.4	$3656.0	$4415.5
TOTAL (1986 dollars)	3184.8	3939.5	3713.7	3311.4	-	-
TITLE IIA Training adults and youth	1414.6	1886.2	1886.2	1783.1	1840.0	1783.0
TITLE IIB Summer youth employment	824.5	824.5	724.5	636.0	750.0	800.0
TITLE III Dislocated workers	94.3	223.0	222.5	95.7	200.0	980.0
TITLE IV Job Corps	414.9	599.2	617.0	612.5	656.4	651.7
Indians	46.7	62.2	62.2	59.6	61.5	58.8
Migrants	45.3	65.5	60.4	57.8	59.6	57.1
Veterans	7.3	9.7	9.7	9.3	10.1	10.0
Research and demonstration projects	46.3	61.7	61.1	59.6	78.5	74.9

Source: Congressional appropriations

increase JTPA appropriations by nearly $800 million for 1988, primarily for assistance to dislocated workers.

Appropriations for employment and training would have been reduced even more drastically had Congress fully accepted budget proposals introduced during the first term of the Reagan administration. As is true for other social programs, the administration has not moved as aggressively against job training assistance in its second term. However, until 1987 the administration continually pressed for large reductions in the Job Corps and the summer youth employment program.

Charges that JTPA administrators have failed to spend funds appropriated by Congress are valid for the dislocated worker program, although the states have begun to address the problem. Laggard spending for dislocated workers led Congress to acquiesce to Reagan administration budget cuts of more than 50 percent for 1986. However, the proportion of other appropriated funds spent during JTPA's first three years is not much different from CETA's initial experience, as follows:

Program	Proportion of appropriated funds spent	
	CETA	JTPA
Training adults and youth	94%	88%
Summer youth employment	86	95
Dislocated workers	NA	66

A closer examination of the Title IIA program shows that state spending difficulties are not confined to the dislocated worker program. While overall Title IIA spending accounts for 88 percent of the appropriated funds, the states only spent 61 percent of their IIA allocations (the localities spent 95 percent). JTPA's record on spending summer youth program funds is better than CETA's, primarily because localities now have more advance notice on the amount of funding they will receive.

Although greater advance notice has promoted program stability, the criteria chosen by Congress to distribute JTPA funds to states and localities has caused serious operational problems. The Labor Department allocates two-thirds of state and local funds based on the distribution of unemployment, and the remainder according to the distribution of the low income population. Two unemployment-based indices count equally in the formula. The first is the relative number of unemployed individuals living in areas with over 6.5 percent unemployment. Governors and local service delivery areas (SDAs) have considerable discretion in defining the boundaries of these areas, allowing them to engage in gerrymandering to maximize their allocation. The second unemployment factor in the formula is the relative number of individuals in the state or service delivery area in excess of a 4.5 percent unemployment rate. To prevent large year-to-year funding reductions due to fluctuations in unemployment rates, the states — but initially not the local service delivery areas — were guaranteed 90 percent of their allotment percentage from the previous year.

The JTPA distribution formula is flawed in several respects, but some of the deficiencies cannot be remedied without costly revisions to the Census Bureau's data collection system. JTPA eligibility is largely restricted to the poor, but the allocation method is heavily influenced by unemployment, which is not a prerequisite for program assistance. In fact, the overlap between these two groups is limited. In 1980, only a fifth of the unemployed were poor, and a similarly small proportion of the poor were unemployed. A majority of the working-age poor were classified as outside the labor force. Consequently, regions with relatively high unemployment rates receive disproportionately greater JTPA funding, even if their share of the poverty population is relatively low (table 2.2).

Table 2.2
The Midwest receives more than its fair share of JTPA funds,
while the South and West are underfunded.

	TITLE IIA Training disadvantaged adults and youth		TITLE IIB Summer Youth Program	
	1985 funding	Low income (16-65)	1985 funding	Low income (16-21)
South	33%	36%	32%	37%
Midwest	28	23	28	23
Northeast	19	21	22	20
West	19	21	18	21

Sources: U.S. Department of Labor and Abt Associates Inc.

For the same reason, urban areas (over 200,000 persons) receive much less than their fair share of Title II funds, rural locales receive proportionate assistance, while the suburbs are overfunded.[4]

The volatility of unemployment rates introduced much instability in year-to-year funding levels. The greatest fluctuations occurred during the transition from CETA to JTPA. Despite JTPA's much-reduced financing, the formula provided some states with more money than they received under CETA. The Midwest region improved its position relative to the rest of the country, while eastern states suffered the largest proportional reductions.[5] Large year-to-year changes continued under JTPA. Although overall Title IIA funding remained fairly constant from 1986 to 1987, 10 states received increases of over 10 percent due to the formula, and 15 states lost the maximum of 10 percent permitted by law. Localities faced even larger yearly allocation fluctuations, ranging from a 52 percent loss to an 85 percent gain across service delivery areas in 1986.[6] To limit reductions, Congress, in 1986, applied the 90 percent hold-harmless rule used for the states to the SDAs, starting with 1987.

The data used to determine the distribution of funds are flawed or dated. The Current Population Survey sample is adequate to yield reasonable unemployment estimates for the most populous states, but too small to reliably indicate unemployment at the SDA level. The 1980 census is used to determine the distribution of the economically disadvantaged population. While the census provides considerably more reliable estimates of the distribution of poverty than sample surveys, new data will not become available until 1992.

To promote geographical equity and year-to-year program stability, Congress could change the allocation formula by giving less weight to unemployment due to its volatility and the unreliability of the data, and by replacing the 4.5 and 6.5 percent thresholds in the current law with the total unemployment count. The distribution of poor persons, representing JTPA's clientele, should be accorded greater weight in the formula. While census poverty data tend to become dated as the decade progresses, they are a far more reliable measure of the distribution of poverty than the Current Population Survey data.

Governors are required to allocate 78 percent of their state Title IIA grant to the SDAs according to the formula; Congress allotted

the remaining 22 percent to governors to promote both state
leadership and coordination between JTPA and other social programs. The state share is divided into four "set-asides," as follows:

- 8 percent for coordination of education programs with JTPA;
- 6 percent for performance awards, technical assistance, and
  incentive awards to encourage assistance to individuals most in
  need;
- 5 percent for state administration; and
- 3 percent for older worker programs (figure 2.1).

Another critical federal responsibility is ensuring that JTPA
funds are properly spent. The Single Audit Act of 1984 permitted
local governments to submit a single audit of expenditures of *all*
federal program funds. Under the new law, JTPA grants receive
much less intense scrutiny than did CETA funds. While auditors
reviewed all CETA finances, accountants operating under the Single
Audit Act only investigate a sample of transactions involving
federal funds. Because JTPA funds account for a fraction of total
federal grants to localities, SDA transactions may not even be
examined by auditors.

Figure 2.1
Allocation of Title IIA funds to states and service
delivery areas (1987).

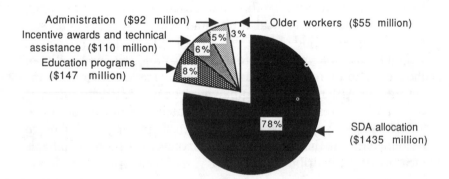

Source: 1987 JTPA appropriation

Although auditors have questioned or disallowed few JTPA expenditures, states and localities have expressed concern over audits and liability for disallowed costs. The Labor Department's refusal to issue JTPA audit guidelines has made states and localities apprehensive that they will be judged by ex post facto standards. The Employment and Training Administration contends that audit guidelines would amount to excessive "back door" regulation of JTPA, thereby inhibiting local autonomy. Ironically, ETA's decision has *increased* paperwork and discouraged local innovation in providing services. To protect themselves against possible disallowed costs, states and SDAs compile extensive documentation justifying outlays. The Labor Department acknowledges these negative results but has not taken corrective action, despite the fact that state and local governments have urged the department to reverse its policies.[7]

The General Accounting Office has also criticized the department's failure to establish accounting and internal controls which ensure that funds are properly spent. GAO concluded that the Labor Department's exclusive reliance on state and local fiscal oversight does not meet the requirements of the Financial Integrity Act, an interpretation rejected by the department.[8]

Technical Assistance

The Labor Department abandoned attempts to improve federal technical assistance undertaken during CETA's last years, and reduced funding from $15 million in 1980 to $5.9 million for 1987. At a time when states and localities critically needed and sought help in implementing the new program, the Labor Department absolved itself of responsibility, impairing JTPA's effectiveness. The department regarded two decades of federal experience administering employment programs as irrelevant to JTPA, and responded to requests for even minimal information with a repeated refrain: "Read the law, ask the governor." Inadequate technical assistance was a serious problem during CETA, but the degree of federal neglect in the early years of JTPA was unprecedented. Despite some improvements, laissez-faire policies have continued under Secretary Brock, who told a group of local business leaders in 1985, "We can't tell you [how to improve JTPA]. You have to tell us."[9]

Almost all technical assistance is provided through subcontractors (nearly two-fifths of the funds have been allocated to the National Alliance of Business alone) rather than directly by the department. This policy is deficient in several important respects. Subcontractors can offer advice but not definitive policy guidance. SDAs seeking assistance must contact a variety of organizations, and are typically charged a fee. Finally, the department's policy prevents the establishment of a permanent federal staff of technical assistance experts.

Data Collection and Analysis

To determine JTPA's effectiveness and improve performance, it is necessary to collect and analyze reliable program information. Federal performance on data collection has been severely deficient, impeding the implementation of viable performance standards and making objective assessments of JTPA difficult.

SDAs are required to complete a semiannual report on Title II expenditures and an annual report on participant characteristics and outcomes. The administrative data provide an overview of JTPA, but do not permit a detailed analysis of services and outcomes for various enrollees. For example, the data do not disaggregate the length of training received by dropouts and those with some college education. To provide more detailed information on JTPA operations, the Labor Department's job training longitudinal survey collects more extensive data on over 12,000 participants from 141 of the 620 SDAs.

In 1986, the Labor Department improved the data collection system. During the first three years, the administrative surveys required no information on the postprogram experiences of JTPA's participants. In direct violation of the law (Section 106), the Office of Management and Budget prevented the Labor Department from collecting information on the posttraining experiences of enrollees until 1986. While augmenting the administrative surveys, the Labor Department scaled back the job training longitudinal survey. In 1986 the department reduced the survey sample from 24,000 to 12,000 participants, and eliminated a longitudinal survey of a 10,000 person subsample.

The overall data collection system has improved, but remains seriously deficient. As a General Accounting Office representative observed during a 1986 congressional hearing, "We have never been able to get adequate information at the local level to answer this key question: 'What kind of people get what kind of training and what kind of outcome do they have in the labor market?' "[10] One fundamental problem is that in the absence of standardized terminology, meaningful comparisons among localities are impossible. The definitions of job placement and training duration are especially deficient, making it difficult to assess the quality or intensity of the services participants receive. The Labor Department draws no distinction between full or part-time, or temporary or permanent jobs, and thus an SDA may report a trainee placed for one day as a successful termination. The length of training is determined by counting the number of calendar days between entering and leaving the program. Localities commonly retain individuals on the rolls for 90 days after completion of training in a "holding status" in order to maximize the SDA's job placement rate. Until 1986 the SDAs were allowed to count the holding period as part of the training. Another important drawback is the failure of SDAs to record cost information which would permit cost-benefit analysis of various forms of assistance.[11]

The halving of the job training longitudinal survey's sample size will render the survey less useful than previously, according to the GAO, precluding analysis for such important groups as high school dropouts.[12] Discarding the Census Bureau's longitudinal survey means abandoning the only source of information on the long-term experiences of JTPA participants. Moreover, despite a significant investment, the Labor Department has yet to release any information from the survey, partly because the Census Bureau did not provide the department with the data until confidentiality concerns were resolved in 1987. The department expects to publish the initial findings from the survey in 1988.

On the positive side, the addition of a postprogram administrative survey will improve JTPA's data collection somewhat. Three months after leaving the program, a sample of participants will be questioned about their employment status, weekly earnings, and number of weeks worked in the three-month period. However, three months is an insufficient period to gauge JTPA's impact, and the survey's reliability is diminished because the Labor Department does not plan to institute quality control reviews. Nor has the department allocated additional funds to SDAs to conduct the assessments. After a two-year grace period during which 6 percent set-aside funds (for performance awards and technical assistance) may be tapped for postprogram follow-ups, the SDAs will be required to utilize their limited administrative funds to cover the cost of the surveys.

Research and Evaluation

The Labor Department is required to submit to Congress an annual assessment of JTPA which incorporates research and evaluation findings. Until 1987, the department ignored this statutory requirement, and there is no record that Congress ever prompted the department to fulfill its responsibility. Adjusted for inflation, the employment and training research budget declined by three-quarters between 1980 and 1987 (figure 2.2). Responding to Secretary Brock's recommendation, Congress boosted ETA's research support by 50 percent to $54 million for 1987. Brock proposed to further increase the research budget to $62 million for 1988.

Figure 2.2
Funding of R&D dropped sharply under JTPA.

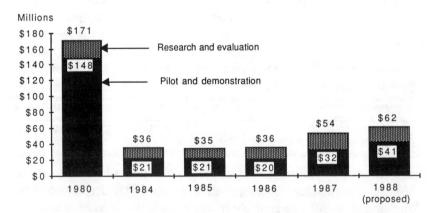

Source: U.S. Department of Labor, Employment and Training Administration

Less than half of ETA's research and evaluation financing has been devoted to analyses of JTPA. Pilot and demonstration funding serves a variety of purposes in addition to research, including employment assistance for the handicapped and technical assistance for organizations which assist minority groups. During JTPA's first three years, most pilot and demonstration funds were provided to the following entities:

Groups serving the handicapped	$12.0 million
National Alliance of Business	10.2
AFL-CIO Human Resources	
Development Institute	5.6
70001 Training and Employment Institute	4.5
Opportunities Industrialization Centers	
of America, Inc.	3.6
National Tooling and Machining	3.5
SER-Jobs for Progress, Inc.	2.6
U.S. Department of Health	
and Human Services	2.4
National Urban League	1.5
National Puerto Rican Forum	1.4

Because of inadequate funding as well as an inefficient allocation of the available research money, major gaps exist in our knowledge of JTPA operations. ETA only recently issued minimal information about the Title IIB summer youth employment program. Two major field studies examined Title IIA, but covered similar ground and left important aspects of the program unstudied. Both scrutinized JTPA's state and local administrative agencies, but neither directly examined the role and activities of subcontractors who provide the training, or the individuals who receive it.[13] Since the administrative agencies infrequently provide services directly to enrollees, the failure to examine service providers is a glaring deficiency in the Labor Department's assessment of JTPA. Consequently, little is known about the providers of training, their quality, the criteria used to accept or reject applicants, and the factors responsible for success or failure. Absent such knowledge, it is difficult to gauge JTPA's success or improve the program.

To fill the informational gaps, the Labor Department opted in 1986 for randomly assigning a sample of individuals eligible for JTPA to either a treatment group or a control group receiving no services. This approach has conceptual appeal, but the department has had considerable difficulty in implementing the project, and the SDAs could not be chosen by a random selection process as originally intended. The experimental sites should begin enrolling participants in 1988, but the results will not be available for several years.

The Absence of Leadership

Despite improvements under Secretary Brock, federal administration of JTPA continues to be dominated by the idea that states and localities know best, and that Washington can contribute most by staying out of the way. As an Ohio JTPA administrator observed, "The Feds are determined to push decisions to the state level, even when a national policy guideline would eliminate confusion."[14] The administration has paid insufficient attention to local requests for audit guidance and improved technical assistance and data collection. As subsequently demonstrated, the vacuum created by federal negligence has not been filled by JTPA's remaining partners.

State Governments

JTPA relies heavily upon the states to exercise administrative authority over job training. The governor is responsible for designating local service delivery areas (SDAs), reviewing local training plans, enforcing performance standards, allocating the portion of Title II funds which are not distributed on a formula basis to SDAs, auditing SDA expenditures, providing technical assistance, and coordinating JTPA operations with the activities of other social programs in the state.

Labor Department or gubernatorial rhetoric notwithstanding, there is little evidence that states have rushed in to exercise their statutory responsibilities, or that state leadership has produced significant results. One easily quantifiable indicator of interest is state cash contributions to JTPA operations. On that score state involvement has been generally negligible or nonexistent. Moreover, the average state has spent less than two-thirds of its federally-provided set-aside funds (for administration, education, performance awards, and older workers). The inability of states to fully spend federally-provided funds has been observed in other programs besides JTPA. On the whole, state policy is limited largely to fulfilling the minimum requirements of the law, although states such as California and Massachusetts have taken a considerably more active stance. An SDA official from Baltimore, Maryland echoed the views of many local officials across the country in observing, "The state has not established any program priorities."[15] The partnership which Congress envisioned between the governor, the newly-created state advisory council, the legislature, business, labor, and other state governmental agencies has emerged only in isolated cases. With few exceptions, state legislatures have demonstrated little interest in JTPA. State agencies, public interest groups and unions play a barely noticeable role in fashioning state policy, and business involvement at the state level has been exercised through the statutorily-required councils which have displayed little initiative.

Governors and State Agencies

The law leaves governors considerable freedom in directing JTPA. Because JTPA state councils are advisory bodies and are barred by law from operating training programs, governors had to designate administrative agencies to manage JTPA at the state level. State JTPA administration is largely an extension of previous CETA arrangements. In four of five states, the former CETA balance-of-state agency (which administered programs not under local control, normally political jurisdictions with less than 100,000 persons) continued to administer JTPA. Only èight states selected new administrative agencies. A majority of governors designated either their labor departments or employment and training agencies to administer all JTPA funds, while about a dozen governors housed JTPA in economic, community affairs or human resource agencies, and even a private corporation. The average state administrative agency employs 33 professional JTPA staff (full-time equivalent positions), ranging from 1 to 157.

The highest initial gubernatorial priority was to disassociate JTPA from CETA's negative image. Following JTPA's implementation, direct gubernatorial involvement became sporadic and administrative authority shifted to the governors' appointees. Given the divergent interests of other actors on the state stage — the legislature, state JTPA councils, other state agencies, business and labor, and community-based organizations — some conflict was natural, but fairly stable relationships ensued following the initial turf battles.[16]

State Councils

Congress charged the job training coordinating councils with advising the governor on the designation of service delivery areas, planning the distribution of funds not allocated by formula to SDAs, monitoring the consistency of local training plans with the state plan, reviewing state employment service and vocational education plans, and preparing an annual report. The councils are also responsible for preparing the required biennial governor's state job training plan, which establishes criteria for coordinating JTPA programs with other state and local education and training efforts, including vocational education, economic development, rehabilitation, and employment service activities. The federal Labor Department can reject the state plan only if it conflicts with the law.

JTPA requires that the following groups be represented on the council:

- one-third from the business community;
- one-fifth from the state legislature and state agencies;
- one-fifth from local governments, including service delivery areas; and
- one-fifth from organized labor, community-based organizations, local educational agencies, and the general public.

Since the quotas do not total 100 percent, governors possess some leeway to favor the representation of particular groups. Gubernatorial appointments to the councils, which average 32 members, have generally met JTPA's requirements.

Constituencies	Proportion
Business	37%
Local governments	19
State agencies	15
State legislatures	6
Local education agencies	6
Community-based organizations	5
Labor unions	5
General public	6

Despite their authorized wide-ranging responsibilities, the councils generally exercise little influence over state JTPA policy. As a rule, councils reinforce state JTPA agency policy rather than acting as an independent force. Analysts examining 20 state councils found that only four councils played a primary role in determining state JTPA policy.[17] One of four SDA administrators and PIC chairpersons believes that the councils have no impact on the program.[18]

Few states provide adequate support for their councils. In 1985 the average council budget was about $275,000, ranging from $50,000 to over $1 million. Only eight councils select their own staff director; the other directors are appointed by the governor or the state administrative agency. The average council has only 3.5 full-time employees, ranging from zero (in eight states) to 12 positions. Only 15 councils have permanent staffs; the others borrow staff from the state JTPA administrative agency.

Legislatures

State legislators have also played a minor role in JTPA, and the few instances where legislators showed an interest in the program were as likely as not to result in unproductive turf battles. Total state appropriations for employment and training programs have accounted for a minute fraction of the federal contribution. The Congressional Budget Office noted that the states spent only $122 million for job training in 1984, less than 5 percent of the federal funds.[19] Incomplete evidence indicates that state contributions have not significantly increased since 1984.

The law requires SDAs to submit local job training plans to state legislatures, but many SDAs fail to do so. Just as Congress failed for years to note that the Labor Department did not submit required annual reports, the state solons have apparently not missed the local plans, according to the National Conference of State Legislatures.

One analyst concluded that only one of five state legislatures demonstrates more than minimal interest in JTPA. The most prominent example is California, which set aside $6 million of its federal social services block grant to match SDA child care assistance, and enacted a new state welfare initiative emphasizing legislative oversight of JTPA services.[20] In addition, California's Employment and Training Panel, with an annual $50 million budget, administers a retraining program for individuals eligible for unemployment insurance. Delaware enacted a similar program on a smaller scale. State commitment even in these cases, however, involves little or no direct appropriation. Both the California and Delaware training programs were financed by reallocating state unemployment insurance funds, and represent no additional financial commitment.

The State-Local Partnership

Conflicts between the federal government and local training administrators were common during CETA. In contrast, analysts have observed little discord between state and SDA officials. However, this relative amity has not markedly improved program management relative to CETA. The states are generally more interested in protecting themselves from audit disallowances than in improving the quality of training.

Following JTPA's enactment in October 1982, governors moved slowly to implement the new law. Understandably not convinced that the Labor Department would relinquish its regulatory role, governors delayed involvement in JTPA administration until the Labor Department issued regulations confirming the federal government's abdication of authority.

State-local JTPA relations have been influenced by the statutorily-defined role of each partner, the federal government's neglect of its responsibilities, and the degree of state activism and SDA sophistication. The law clearly reserves most training decisions to the SDAs, but Congress empowered the states to influence local program operations by other means. The states may establish educational requirements for local programs, add to or modify federal performance standards, and define key terms such as what constitutes a job placement. In addition, JTPA discretionary set-aside funds can be used as a carrot to encourage desirable SDA behavior. The federal noninterventionist posture further expanded state authority by default.

Most states did not choose to exercise their full authority. State review of local training plans was characterized as "a paper policy process devoid of any real policy oversight" by a Lexington, Kentucky SDA administrator, a view endorsed by many local officials. Although the Labor Department delegated the interpretation of the law to the states, these often behaved as if they had been passed a hot potato. A Des Moines, Iowa SDA official noted critically, "The state has been reluctant to provide necessary interpretation of the act and in many cases has allowed localities to struggle through court proceedings and binding arbitration."[21]

Prior job training experience was another important factor in the evolution of state-local relations. The geographic boundaries of half the SDAs are virtually identical to the CETA prime sponsors, and because these SDAs had considerably more familiarity with job training programs than the states, they were often able to limit state intervention. SDA officials further expanded their influence through statewide associations. By mid-1985 virtually all states with more than two SDAs had SDA directors' organizations, and several had associations of PIC officials.

Both the degree of state activism, and the problems between states and SDAs, can be gleaned by examining the SDA designation process and state technical assistance policies. Congress authorized governors to set the geographical boundaries of local program areas. Since it was widely believed that 470 CETA prime sponsors was an excessive number, the designers of JTPA anticipated that governors would consolidate local operations. Instead, the number of SDAs ballooned to 620. Several factors caused the proliferation of SDAs. Gubernatorial authority in creating SDAs is somewhat limited. Jurisdictions with over 200,000 people and consortia of local governments serving a substantial portion of a labor market area with more than 200,000 persons have the right to form an SDA. Another factor was that local governments were often able to pressure governors into designating them as separate SDAs and avoid consolidation with other areas. Since governors had little to gain politically from opposing local interests, they often acquiesced to lobbying pressures. In fact, most of the increase in SDAs was attributable to the subdivision of former CETA balance-of-state areas.[22]

The proliferation of SDAs resulted in programs of less than optimal size and the wasteful duplication of administrative resources. JTPA's significantly lower budget exacerbates this problem. Over a quarter of the SDAs receive less than $1 million, considered minimal to administer a job training program. Based on average outlays per enrollee and the duration of training provided by SDAs, a $1 million annual allocation permits services to only about 550 participants, with only slightly more than 100 individuals enrolled at any given time. Since about a third of these participants enroll in classroom training, providing cost-effective training for more than one or two occupations is difficult at best.

State technical assistance is most commonly directed toward management information, performance standards, youth employment programs, and the analysis of labor market information to identify growth occupations. SDAs commonly complain about inadequate state technical assistance. Despite inadequate technical assistance at the federal level, a Toledo, Ohio PIC representative observed, "The state does not have the same quality of staff that the federal government has available to it. Often the SDA ends up providing on-the-job training to the state."[23] State administrative agencies, which provide most technical assistance, on average assign only three staff members to this task. In fact, 11 administrative staffs surveyed did not have a single technical assistance specialist.[24] Most assistance is funded by the JTPA set-aside which provides 6 percent of Title IIA funds (a little over $100 million annually) to governors for technical assistance and performance awards. However, in JTPA's first three years, the states spent only a third of the available 6 percent funds, and only a little over a third of the expenditures were devoted to technical assistance.[25]

Little Ventured, Little Gained

Driven by ideology rather than the knowledge gained from research or experience, policymakers during the early 1980s acted as if all wisdom resided in state houses and the federal government could do little right. But since JTPA's enactment, most states have passively waited for federal instruction rather than forging ahead on their own.

Before JTPA, job training expertise was concentrated at the federal and local levels. The states, relatively inexperienced, would have had to invest substantial resources to design and improve training programs for the poor. Instead, most states believe that local administrators know best, and are content to leave well enough alone. Moreover, as the designation of SDAs demonstrated, the states have far less leverage over localities than the drafters of JTPA assumed. The states seem far more interested in boosting local programs than in critically examining them. Ironically, a program which was designed to demonstrate the potential of state leadership instead suggests that a strong federal presence is necessary to administer effective training programs for the unskilled and deficiently educated. While a genuine federal-state partnership would be more desirable, the JTPA experience casts doubt on whether this arrangement can be achieved.

The Local Partnership

Congress expressly delegated training authority to JTPA local service delivery agencies. To promote leadership, cooperation and accountability, Congress instituted a complex administrative framework. Local elected officials, preeminent under CETA, share authority with newly empowered private industry councils, which are dominated by business representatives. They jointly select a program administrator to supervise day-to-day operations and service providers to train enrollees.

Political factors took precedence in the administrative redesign of local training programs. As a Rockford, Illinois SDA official summed up the changes, "I do not feel that the PIC/elected official concept is administratively preferable to the CETA system, but under the circumstances a drastic change was necessary because CETA suffered from a — mostly unwarranted — negative image. The new partnership has allowed the image of employment and training to become more positive."[26] There is little indication that a different administrative framework has significantly improved JT-PA's operations, but the public relations impact has clearly been salutary.

By 1987 the JTPA system was made up of 620 local SDAs, each with an average of about 8-10 staff members. Six governors of states with populations below a million opted for statewide SDAs. At the other extreme, 9 states have over 20 SDAs, topped by California with 51, as follows:

SDAs	States
One each	6
2-5	13
6-10	9
11-15	6
16-20	7
Over 20	9

One of every four SDAs is an intact political entity — a state, city, or, most commonly, a county; the rest are multiple local political jurisdictions.[27]

The average JTPA Title II grant in 1987 amounted to $3.5 million, ranging for Title IIA operations alone from $67,000 for an Arizona SDA to $56 million for New York City. Two-thirds of the SDAs received less than $2 million for Title IIA operations (figure 2.3). SDAs also receive additional money, mostly from the Title IIA state set-asides and the Title III dislocated worker program, totaling about a tenth of the average SDA's budget according to a 1985 survey.[28]

Private Industry Councils

Employer representatives, who by law must constitute a majority of private industry council members, are appointed by the chief elected officials of the SDA from a list of nominees presented by local business organizations, primarily chambers of commerce.

Figure 2.3
The Title IIA budget of some 400 SDAs was below $2 million (1986).

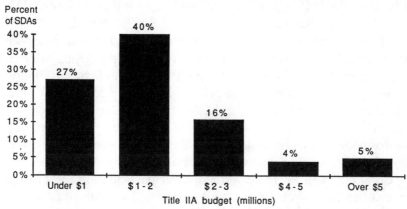

Source: U.S. Department of Labor, Employment and Training Administration

Other PIC members represent local education agencies, the public employment service, labor unions, rehabilitation agencies, community-based organizations, and economic development agencies. The chairperson must be chosen from the business members. The size of the PIC was initially determined by elected officials, but subsequently PIC members determined the council's size. However, the authority to fill vacancies remains with elected officials. The average PIC of 25 members has representatives from the following constituencies:

Business	14
Education institutions	3
Labor unions	2
Community-based organizations	2
Employment service	1
Vocational rehabilitation agencies	1
Economic development agencies	1
Other	1

Initially, few PIC members possessed experience with federal employment and training programs: only a quarter had served on a

CETA council. Although direct information is available only for PIC chairpersons, probably many PIC members had garnered considerable experience with JTPA by 1987. Over 90 percent of the chairpersons have served more than two years on a council. Overall PIC turnover is low, averaging about five members per year. SDA administrative personnel supply the staff for 70 percent of PICs.[29]

PICs focus their attention on the selection and review of service providers. Since business representatives constitute a majority of PIC members, it is not surprising that PICs tend to favor on-the-job training and to frown upon services which increase costs, such as child care assistance or stipends. Curriculum reviews and on-site inspections usually play no part in PIC judgments.[30] Emphasis on performance standards reflects both the Labor Department's priorities and a business predilection for bottom-line judgments.

Congress expected increased employer participation in JTPA to reap a rich harvest of benefits, and the Labor Department as well as many SDAs regard business involvement as the key to the program's claimed success. The Reagan administration views business as inherently more efficient than government, but support for employer participation in JTPA has extended beyond those who promote it as a matter of faith. Since most jobs are generated in the private sector, it seems only reasonable that businesses have a voice in employment and training efforts. Business leadership is not considered as susceptible to constituent pressures as elected officials, and hence freer to make program decisions on professional grounds. Finally, JTPA's designers hoped that greater business involvement would expand training opportunities and boost job placements.

The expansion of the employer role in job training programs was implemented largely without controversy. As Congress intended, business members dominate most PICs, and they share the direction of SDAs with elected officials. While business participation is not as critical to JTPA's workings as the Reagan administration contends, increased employer involvement remains a notable political achievement.

One area where business has clearly made a difference is in JTPA's image. To some extent business had no choice but to promote JTPA. The Reagan administration and business organizations sold JTPA as a training program run by employers dedicated

to the "bottom line," rather than by "do gooders." This character-
ization of the program is vastly exaggerated, but it effectively
co-opted the most vocal former critics of employment and training
programs. PIC public relations activities also undoubtedly contribute to JTPA's positive image.

About half of PIC leaders either train or hire JTPA participants;
the others who do not cite an absence of openings or a need for
more skilled workers than the program can provide. Some observers argue that conflict of interest laws deter PIC representatives
from training or hiring JTPA participants in their own firms, but
less than one of seven PIC chairpersons offered this explanation for
not training JTPA enrollees.

To date, employers have maintained a strong interest in JTPA.
Of the average 14 PIC business members, about four leave per year.
The primary reasons offered by a sample of PIC chairpersons were
personal factors and the amount of time required. Most PICs have
no problems recruiting new business members, and the time commitment is the major difficulty for PICs which have such problems.
Surveys of PIC chairpersons and SDA administrators also show
that almost all PIC employer representatives are satisfied with their
role and influence in JTPA.[31]

One analysis concluded that no significant operational differences
distinguish PIC versus government-dominated SDAs. The movement toward increased utilization of on-the-job training under
JTPA was not more pronounced in PIC-dominated SDAs, and
where the public sector was preeminent there was no greater
tendency to serve a more severely disadvantaged clientele. The
analysts also found no consistent differences in performance
outcomes.[32] Surveys of SDA officials also indicate that the views of
PIC employer representatives and their fellow council members are
not markedly different. Only slightly more than half of PIC
chairpersons and SDA administrators thought the attitudes of the
two groups diverged, and no more than a fifth pointed to any single
issue differentiating business and nonbusiness PIC members. Surprisingly, only a fifth of the SDA administrators thought employer
members were more responsive to business needs than other PIC
representatives. JTPA's meager resources and the Labor Depart-

ment's emphasis on performance standards may more significantly influence program operations than the enhanced business role.

Apart from PIC involvement, local businesses also contribute modest financial and other support to SDA programs. Two-thirds of the SDAs receive some form of material assistance from local businesses, most commonly training or office equipment. Assistance in developing training curricula, office or classroom space, and training personnel are donated to about 30 percent of the SDAs. One in five SDAs is aided by nontraining personnel (e.g., computer programmers or accountants) from local firms. One in six SDAs receives business cash contributions, averaging $17,000 (ranging from $1000 to $1 million), but this represents less than 0.1 percent of federal expenditures.[33]

The Partnership in Action

To ensure that employers would be equal partners in formulating SDA policy, Congress divided authority between PICs and local officials. The local partnership jointly selects an administrative agency to run the program. Government bodies, primarily local governments, account for nearly two-thirds of program administrators. Most of the remaining SDAs are administered by PICs or private nonprofit groups (figure 2.4). Administrative changes since

Figure 2.4
Local governments administered half of SDAs (1985).

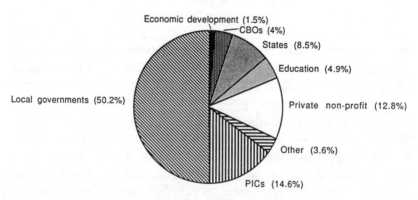

Economic development (1.5%)
CBOs (4%)
States (8.5%)
Education (4.9%)
Local governments (50.2%)
Private non-profit (12.8%)
Other (3.6%)
PICs (14.6%)

Source: National Alliance of Business

1983 show a decreasing use of local governments and an increased utilization of nonprofit organizations. From 1983 to 1985 the proportion of local governments selected as administrative agencies declined from 57.1 to 50.2 percent, while the proportion of nonprofit administrative agencies nearly tripled, rising from 4.5 to 12.8 percent.[34]

The local biennial training plan requires the approval of PICs and elected officials, and subsequent substantial deviations from the plan also require joint approval. The plan must include a detailed presentation of the type, duration and cost of the training; the performance goals; the means of selecting service providers; financial accountability safeguards; and the means of coordinating JTPA with other employment-related programs. The governor may reject or amend the plan for the following reasons:

- the plan does not comply with JTPA's provisions or regulations;
- inadequate safeguards exist to protect funds;
- the administrative agency does not have the capacity to operate the program;
- the local plan does not comply with the coordination criteria enumerated in the governor's plan; or
- measures to correct audit or performance standards problems are inadequate.

Disputes between the governor and the SDA are resolved by the federal Secretary of Labor. Whether the plans represent a serious effort to achieve local goals, or are prepared merely to conform with the law, is a matter of speculation. State reviews of local plans are generally pro forma; rejection of local plans is apparently rare, since no cases have been reported.[35]

Observers do not agree on the general balance of authority which evolved during the program's first four years. Although the consensus is that the PICs play an important policymaking role, the extent of PIC dominance varies. JTPA's provisions made it inevitable that the role of elected officials and job training staff would significantly diminish under JTPA compared with CETA. In addition, many local officials lost interest in employment and training programs after funding declined and public service jobs were eliminated. The money and extra staff associated with CETA had enabled elected officials to expand public services and thus enhance their political prestige. Another factor which facilitates PIC authority is a belief among many elected officials that the councils will shield them from blame in the event of fraud or abuse.

Few instances of confrontation have surfaced between PICs and elected officials. In many cases where the PICs determine local policy, elected officials either voluntarily acquiesce to PIC dominance or actively promote PIC authority. Only in isolated cases has business hostility toward former CETA administrative holdovers been a problem. Conflict between elected officials of multijurisdictional SDAs occurs about as often as PIC/elected officials disputes.[36] Despite their diminished authority, three of five city officials surveyed by the National League of Cities said they were satisfied with their role in JTPA (the remainder felt they had too little voice in the program).[37]

Elected officials are better able to dominate SDAs in highly rural and major urban areas. In the former, geographically dispersed council membership makes active PIC participation difficult to achieve. In major urban areas, mayors generally tend to wield much greater local authority than elected officials in less populous jurisdictions, and administrative sponsorship of long-standing programs is difficult to overturn. Interestingly, the elected officials of single-jurisdiction SDAs are not necessarily better able than leaders of multiple jurisdictions to set JTPA policy. In fact, in some cases competition for JTPA funds in multijurisdictional SDAs produces agreements between public officials that effectively preclude PIC control. This occurred even in one SDA composed of 86 political jurisdictions.[38]

Congress obviously intended the JTPA administrative structure to improve employment and training performance. Although it is difficult to isolate the impact of a different administrative system from other program changes, several tentative conclusions emerge from JTPA's first four years. Whether or not the system is superior to CETA's prime sponsor network, the JTPA structure clearly represents a viable administrative framework. PIC relations with elected officials are generally harmonious. However, budget reductions, limitations on stipends for trainees, and the introduction of performance standards (especially job placement and cost-per-placement criteria) probably exercise greater influence on JTPA operations than the new local administrative arrangement. Business participation has significantly enhanced JTPA's image, but there is no definitive evidence that employer involvement has improved program operations.

Coordination

Convinced that divided authority and rivalry among government agencies impeded cost-effective assistance to the poor, JTPA's authors required governors to integrate JTPA with local education and training, public assistance, employment service, rehabilitation, and economic development agencies. Such efforts were not new, but Congress made coordination an integral part of JTPA and allocated funds to achieve this goal.

Better-integrated programs provide obvious benefits. The sense of futility and powerlessness which often accompanies poverty is reinforced when applicants are shuffled amongst various agencies. Increased coordination offers job training administrators operating with reduced federal funding a potentially important means to tap into other federally- and state-funded programs to enhance training and employment opportunities for JTPA clients.

Effective coordination requires diverse strategies. Referring AFDC applicants to JTPA may facilitate coordination, but more complicated financial agreements are required when local SDAs contract with public employment service offices and vocational education agencies to provide placement assistance and classroom training. However, in these examples SDAs would still be using established institutions in a traditional manner. It is more difficult to persuade established institutions to alter their operations to serve JTPA's aims. For example, state economic development programs often entice businesses to relocate by offering generous tax and other incentives. Asking firms to hire poor, unemployed job seekers is hardly an inducement, making coordination between JTPA and conventional economic development programs difficult.

Prior to JTPA, ad hoc efforts to integrate employment and training services with other social programs had produced few notable results. JTPA attempted to improve this record by making state councils responsible for developing coordination initiatives and subsequently monitoring progress. Governors may reject SDA plans which do not conform with state coordination goals, and also control discretionary coordination funds. A portion of the funds from three of the state set-asides can be used to bolster coordination efforts.

State set-asides	1987 allocation
	(millions)
Education (8 percent)	$147
Incentive awards and	
technical assistance (6 percent)	110
Older worker training programs (3 percent)	55

JTPA also amended the Wagner-Peyser and Social Security Acts to promote coordination of job training with the employment service and the Work Incentive program for AFDC recipients. In addition, governors may allocate 10 percent of employment service funds — nearly $80 million in 1987 — to operate joint employment service/ JTPA projects.

Employment Service

Established in 1933, the federal-state employment service system attempts to match employers with job seekers — many of them disadvantaged — through a nationwide network of over 2000 public employment offices with a $778 million budget for 1987. The expansion of public service employment during the Carter administration encouraged coordination between the employment service and employment and training programs. As long as local CETA administrators were not held accountable for ineligible public workers recruited through public employment offices, and the latter received credit for placing CETA enrollees, both agencies profited by cooperating. However, publicized charges that ineligible persons were hired to fill public service employment slots caused Congress to tighten monitoring. Local programs were held strictly account-

able for ineligible enrollees, and consequently reduced subcontract-
ing to employment offices and handled eligibility determinations
internally. Two-thirds of CETA programs in 1980 also utilized
public employment offices to help CETA trainees find jobs, but
three-fifths of local CETA administrators thought public employment offices performed this task poorly, and some stopped referring
enrollees to the employment service.[39]

Because of the close connection between the employment service
and JTPA's job placement mission, Congress required local public
employment offices to develop their program plans in conjunction
with PICs and elected officials. The three local partners as well as
the state council must approve the plans.

The Reagan administration's decision — going well beyond the
intent of the law — to virtually abandon the employment service to
the states further facilitated gubernatorial authority to coordinate
JTPA and the employment service. While Congress rejected administration proposals to turn over the employment service to the
states, the Secretary of Labor cut federal staff assigned to employment service activities to a score of employees, rendering effective
national oversight impossible. Because local employment offices
have no independent authority, federal nonintervention effectively
gave governors even more control over the employment service than
they have over JTPA.

Despite this expanded authority, governors have generally done
little to reshape the public employment service, and have displayed
little interest in doing so. Several states have placed the service in the
same agency as JTPA, aligned the local geographical boundaries of
the two programs, or used employment service 10 percent set-aside
funds for coordinated projects.[40] However, a study of 16 states
concluded that governors have little impact on employment service
policy. In fact, analysts considered the state employment service
plans less structured than pre-JTPA plans. State JTPA plans
typically contain only general references to the employment service.
Even merging JTPA and the employment service into the same state
agency does not ensure coordination, because in most cases the
separate programs continue business as usual. For example, Florida, which merged the two organizations at the local level, only

partially improved coordination because the governor exercised little control over local JTPA operations.[41]

At the local level, one study found that only 6 of 31 SDAs examined used the employment service to provide most eligibility determinations. The service is rarely used as the main source for job placements, although this is the agency's primary function. The study also concluded that the PICs had no real impact on local employment office policy in any of the 31 SDAs studied, and remained largely uninterested in improving coordination with public employment offices. In fact, PIC involvement in employment service planning has progressively declined.[42] Two other surveys found that almost all SDAs have written agreements with local employment offices involving applicant intake and job referrals, but these probably represent a continuation of activities initiated during CETA, which required agreements between the two agencies.[43]

Several factors partially explain the lack of interest by most states and localities in coordinating the two programs. State and local employment service offices represent a stable bureaucracy not readily amenable to change, and since the staff are state employees their loyalty lies with state rather than local interests. Second, many administrators believe that the programs serve different ends — training versus direct job placement. Third, the states cannot compel SDAs to utilize the employment service. The 6 percent set-aside can encourage this practice, but these funds are spread thin in attempting to achieve multiple objectives. Finally, JTPA's emphasis on performance standards and performance-based contracting impedes local coordination. Under performance-based contracts, the SDAs withhold full payment until the trainee is placed in a job, and contractors tend to place clients themselves — or claim to have placed them — rather than risk financial losses by relying on public employment offices in which they have little confidence.

Education

A clear dividing line cannot be drawn between education and job training programs; in fact, the latter are often called "second chance" education programs. If U.S. education and economic systems functioned effectively, there would be little need for JTPA, but the persistence of inadequate literacy and vocational skills among millions of adults demonstrates the need for cooperation between the two systems. However, the task is extraordinarily difficult. Americans are educated by a multiplicity of diverse institutions administered by all three levels of government as well as the private sector. Curriculum decisions are made by state agencies as well as 15,000 local school districts. The federal government has expanded its role in education since World War II, but has limited leverage because federal money accounts for less than 9 percent of total spending and Americans have traditionally resisted federal involvement in education.

Prior to JTPA, the most important effort to promote coordination between education and employment and training programs was undertaken through one of the 1977 Youth Employment and Demonstration Projects Act (YEDPA) programs. The youth employment and training program, financed at nearly $600 million annually between 1978 and 1981, required that 22 percent of the funding be spent on joint projects with schools. Evaluations of the effort concluded that cooperation between education and training institutions improved, but this yielded only limited changes in school services to dropouts or approaches toward disadvantaged students. Without direct authority to influence school programming, YEDPA grants offered too little financial clout to effect changes.[44]

The 1917 Vocational Education Act marked the first federal involvement in job training, and today represents an important federal educational investment directly related to JTPA. The program serves primarily noncollege bound students. The fiscal 1987 budget provides $875 million for vocational education, and states and localities spend an additional $7 billion. In 1987 the Reagan administration proposed to eliminate federal support for the program. Approximately 17 million students are enrolled in vocational education programs, although less than 6 million receive occupationally-specific training. Altogether, an estimated 1.3 million disadvantaged youth received at least some assistance from the program.

When federal training programs were inaugurated in the early 1960s, most classroom training was offered in public vocational education facilities. After CETA expanded the range of service providers, the federal government attempted to maintain cooperation between job training and vocational education activities, but with limited success.[45] Tight school budgets impeded coordination efforts, and the back to basics movement deemphasized vocational training.

The 1966 Adult Education Act established the major federal basic education program for disadvantaged adults. It finances literacy training, secondary education, and English as a second language courses with $106 million in fiscal 1987 federal funds and another $175 million from states and localities. Approximately 2.5 million people enroll annually in federally-funded adult education programs, which spend an average of only $112 per participant.

Most of the statutory requirements utilized by JTPA and the 1984 Carl Perkins Vocational Education Act to improve the coordination of job training with education programs were carried over from previous legislation. The JTPA 8 percent set-aside is to be spent through cooperative agreements among state education agencies, SDAs, and local education agencies. At least 80 percent of the grant must be allocated for educational services, and these funds must be matched by the state or locality. Three-quarters of the service funds must be spent on the disadvantaged, with the remainder to be used for other individuals facing barriers to employment. The balance of the education grant is intended to facilitate coordination with job training programs. Another JTPA provision requires SDAs to give education agencies the opportunity to provide training services unless it is demonstrated that other service providers would be more effective.

To date, however, there is little evidence that these statutory requirements have had a measurable impact on program operations. State council administrators surveyed saw few signs of coordination at either the state or the local level. Despite the law's requirement that SDAs be party to the disposition of 8 percent funds, half the states bypass the SDAs.[46] A National Governors' Association survey of 37 states found that only 3 states had appropriated funds for the 8 percent matching requirement (the others presumably made in-kind contributions), and the states have spent only a little over three-fourths of the federal set-aside funds.

Programs financed through the 8 percent education set-aside provide classroom training to roughly 100,000 individuals annually, but only a quarter of participants receive remedial education, English as a second language assistance, or high school equivalency training. The 1986 JTPA amendments require states to serve at least some dropouts with 8 percent funds, but such a minimal standard may not have much impact. Only 32 percent of the terminees found jobs, at hourly wages averaging $5.[47]

Welfare

Congress specified reductions in "welfare dependency" as one of JTPA's principal objectives, continuing a two-decade-old policy of using employment and training programs to promote the self-sufficiency of welfare recipients. JTPA's efforts have been augmented by the Work Incentive (WIN) program, which serves employable Aid to Families with Dependent Children (AFDC) recipients. In fiscal 1987 the appropriation for WIN amounted to $133 million, less than a third of the level appropriated six years earlier in inflation-adjusted dollars.

The 1981 Omnibus Budget Reconciliation Act permitted states flexibility in designing and administering work-welfare programs and to require AFDC recipients to work in return for assistance. Stepping up the pressure to induce AFDC recipients to seek work, the 1982 Tax Equity and Fiscal Responsibility Act allowed the states to require AFDC recipients to participate in a job search program to establish or maintain their eligibility for assistance. While all states operate work or training programs for AFDC recipients, the number actually assisted is unknown. Beginning in 1987, the states must also implement employment and training programs for food stamp recipients. In addition to federally mandated or encouraged programs, some states also provide employment assistance to poor individuals receiving state or local general assistance.

Historically, coordination between WIN and other employment efforts has been minimal.[48] Since JTPA/welfare coordination is apparently not a high state priority — Massachusetts and a few other states are exceptions — it is unlikely that cooperation has increased in recent years.[49] At the local level, few welfare administrators are represented on PICs. Two of every five JTPA participants receive some form of public assistance, nearly identical to the experience under CETA. A survey of 45 SDAs found that two-thirds of the welfare recipients served had not been referred by a welfare agency or any other program. Moreover, only a fourth of the WIN referrals who enrolled in JTPA obtained support services from the WIN program.[50] Given general SDA practices, it is unlikely that these enrollees received support assistance from JTPA funds.

Other factors suggest that coordination between JTPA and welfare programs may have decreased since JTPA's enactment. Where a CETA prime sponsor had to deal with one major federal program (WIN), Congress subsequently created five federal work-welfare programs, undoubtedly complicating both state and local coordination efforts. At the same time, federal funding has dwindled, and the uncertainty of WIN's future hardly provides an impetus for JTPA to invest much effort in cooperating with the program. Finally, although the law requires the Labor Department to ensure that WIN registrants are referred to JTPA, the administration's laissez faire policy toward both programs renders this provision toothless.

A lesser obstacle to coordination is JTPA's requirement that any payments to AFDC recipients be counted as income. Senator Dan Quayle reported that, by requiring agencies to reduce AFDC benefits by the amount of money JTPA enrollees receive to cover travel or other training-related expenses, welfare recipients are discouraged from pursuing training.[51]

Older Workers

On the average, the incidence of unemployment among older individuals is relatively low, but those who lose their jobs tend to remain unemployed longer than younger workers, or drop out of the labor force entirely. Of a state's Title IIA allocation, 3 percent is set aside (a little over $50 million nationally) for services to low income individuals over 55. States pass most 3 percent funds to SDAs.

One of the very few social programs that Congress has singled out for increased funding in the 1980s, the Senior Community Service Employment Program (Title V of the Older Americans Act) is the major employment program for the elderly. The program's budget has risen from $275 million in fiscal 1981 to $326 million in fiscal 1987, almost matching the inflation rate. The Senior Community Service Employment Program annually provides part-time public jobs for approximately 100,000 older individuals in households with incomes below 125 percent of the poverty line. This income criterion is more generous than the JTPA standard.

During JTPA's first three years, the states spent only two-thirds of the 3 percent set-aside. The mandatory allocation of funds for the elderly — which did not exist under CETA — may have improved coordination with the Senior Community Service Employment Program. However, Congress left little room for effective cooperation between the two programs. Nearly 80 percent of the community service program's funds are allocated by the federal government directly to eight national contractors, including the American Association of Retired Persons, the National Council on Aging and the Urban League. Governors have almost no control over this money. Thus whatever coordination occurs is probably due to arrangements made by individual SDAs, but cooperation is undoubtedly limited since the two programs offer different services to their clients.

Three percent set-aside programs enroll about 25,000 individuals annually. The reported characteristics of these enrollees do not differ appreciably from older enrollees in other Title IIA programs. Most 3 percent trainees enroll in brief job search programs, as follows:

Service	Enrollees receiving service
Job search assistance	57%
Classroom training	27
On-the-job training	21
Work experience	8

Since a small proportion of participants receive multiple forms of assistance, the total is slightly higher than 100 percent. Reports from 15 states indicate that 64 percent of terminees found jobs at an average hourly wage of $4.50.[52]

Economic Development

Coordination between JTPA and economic development programs has attracted increasing attention in the employment and training community, although the law itself barely addresses the subject. However, the lip service to economic development has not been matched by action. The few states which attempt to coordinate JTPA with economic development programs tend to tap JTPA 8 percent education set-aside funds. One state targeted all of its 8 percent JTPA set-aside and 10 percent employment service set-aside for economic development projects, and in addition required the SDAs to reserve 10 percent of Title IIA funds for company-specific training. Other means of coordinating the two programs include either reserving a portion of jobs created through economic development projects for JTPA participants, or requiring contractors to use JTPA as a first source in soliciting job applications.[53]

A major obstacle to coordinating JTPA and economic development efforts is the divergent goals of the two programs. Many state economic development policies are characterized by beggar-thy-neighbor efforts to persuade firms to relocate, and requiring employers to hire the poor fits awkwardly into an incentive package. Consequently, a National Governors' Association survey found that only two states had such hiring requirements, and most states volunteered that they would not consider including JTPA training as a carrot for luring employers. The wide range of economic development programs — encompassing grants, loans, loan guarantees, and tax incentives administered by various state agencies — further impedes coordination.[54] Even if potential employers were interested in JTPA trainees, it would be difficult to dovetail the timing of the training with the hiring needs of the employers.

Given the present nature of economic development programs, initiatives to coordinate these programs with JTPA are probably misdirected. Including JTPA as part of an incentive package to woo firms from one state to another is no more than a corporate shell game which wastes scarce dollars available for training.

Great Expectations, Minimal Returns

There is little reason to believe that coordination between job training and other social programs has improved much under JTPA. While conceptually appealing, the importance of coordination has been greatly exaggerated by many program administrators and policymakers. Enhanced coordination can improve program effectiveness, but should never have been expected to mitigate the effects of multibillion dollar budget cuts in employment and training programs.

Promoting cooperation among various social programs is inherently difficult. JTPA administrators have no control over other social programs, and can attempt to facilitate coordination but not mandate it. Responsibility for the different programs lies with various levels of government, and in several programs the private sector plays an important role. In many cases, no single administrator has the authority or capability to compel various agencies to coordinate divergent programs. Even in instances where the state government possesses sufficient statutory authority, longstanding bureaucratic arrangements may effectively block reform.

In addition to difficulties emanating from fragmented administrative responsibility, the purposes, clientele and operations of many social programs differ greatly from JTPA. Common instructional goals characterize vocational education and JTPA, but school financing is not directly dependent on graduates' job placement records. Both JTPA and work-welfare programs emphasize employment results, but most work-welfare programs stress direct job placement activities to remove welfare recipients from the rolls as quickly as possible. Staff have little incentive, therefore, to place a welfare recipient in a JTPA classroom training program rather than directly in a job.

JTPA's coordination provisions are also too ambiguous to ensure results. Compounding the problem, the Labor Department pursues a deliberate nonintervention policy and state coordinative directives are generally vague and inconsequential. Unless Congress articulates clear goals, which are further specified and enforced by federal and state administrators, increased cooperation will remain only a rhetorical objective.

Several key assumptions by JTPA's designers regarding coordination have proven to be erroneous. Elevating the role of states, JTPA relies upon the governors to guarantee better interprogram cooperation, but state agencies do little to promote coordination. Another widely-held misconception was that reduced funding would prompt JTPA administrators to work more closely with other programs and more fully use alternative resources. However, funding and personnel cuts across almost all social programs instead caused widespread retrenchment, and administrators have been reluctant to invest in coordination at the expense of direct provision of services.

Even if the SDAs had desired to pursue coordination efforts more vigorously, JTPA's administrative cost limitations constrain such action. Even without significant investments in coordination and with some creative accounting, the average SDA devotes the maximum allowable funding to administration. Assessing barriers to cooperation, negotiating interagency agreements to eliminate coordinative obstacles, and monitoring progress to ensure smooth implementation require significant resources which would undoubtedly exceed JTPA's administrative cost limitations.

Finaly,Reagan administration efforts to revamp, drastically reduce or abolish a number of programs related to JTPA inhibit interprogram cooperation. Until the future of the employment service, vocational education, and WIN programs becomes clearer, cooperation between these programs and JTPA will be hampered.

3

Training Adults
and Youth

JTPA service delivery area (SDA) operators are permitted broad flexibility in devising training strategies for enrollees, but the law severely limits spending for administration, allowances and other supportive services. The SDAs are also required to meet federal performance standards governing job placement rates, wages, and the cost of providing assistance. JTPA training efforts may be an improvement over CETA in some respects, but the program's problems are serious and remain largely unaddressed.

Enrollees

Eligibility and Selection

As under CETA, eligibility is generally restricted to

- individuals whose families earn less than the federal poverty guideline or less than 70 percent of the Labor Department's lower living standard income level. (The latter guideline varies by locality, ranging in the continental U.S. from $9210 to $11,660 for the average-sized poor household of three, compared to the uniform 1987 federal poverty guideline of $9300.);
- individuals in families receiving cash welfare or food stamps;
- foster children; and
- handicapped adults whose personal earnings do not exceed the income criteria, irrespective of their family's income.

57

Unemployment insurance, cash welfare, and child support payments are not counted as income in determining eligibility. Congress also permitted SDAs to assist individuals who do not meet the income criteria but face other barriers to employment, including displaced homemakers, addicts and school dropouts, but such participants may not exceed 10 percent of total enrollment. However, few SDAs actively utilize this provision.

The law singles out for special assistance subgroups within the poverty population. SDAs are mandated to spend 40 percent of their Title IIA funds on youth enrollees under 22 years old and enroll dropouts and welfare recipients in proportion to their presence in the area's eligible population. Less well-defined is the requirement that JTPA serve "those who can benefit from and who are most in need of" assistance.

Very little is known about how SDAs recruit applicants for the program. Past examinations of CETA and the Job Corps indicate that most job training applicants learned about these programs by word of mouth, and the same is probably true of JTPA.

Deciding who to select from among the applicants is one of the thornier problems facing SDA administrators. The law emphasizes assistance to those "most in need," but the Labor Department has failed to define this ambiguous requirement and consequently most states and SDAs ignore it.[1] Because serving deficiently skilled and educated applicants is costly and fraught with difficulties, local administrators tend to favor more employable individuals in order to show "results." This practice, known in the trade as "creaming," is accomplished by establishing educational and occupational skill qualifications as well as using more informal and subjective assessments of applicants' motivation and employability.

The extent of creaming is difficult to quantify because few SDAs record the number of rejected applicants, let alone the reasons for disqualification. However, every case study of JTPA has found evidence of creaming. In one SDA, 60 percent of the dropouts who applied were turned away. In another, 362 of 1844 eligible applicants were rejected because they were functionally illiterate, needed remedial education, or had a limited command of English. Some SDAs require high school or equivalency diplomas as a prerequisite for enrollment.[2] A comparison between the characteristics of employable AFDC mothers (those required to register for the Work Incentive program) and AFDC mothers enrolled in JTPA also tends to indicate creaming. Only half of the former have a high school degree, compared with two-thirds of the AFDC mothers enrolled in JTPA.[3] Many SDAs also screen out applicants with unsatisfactory work histories or skills. For example, some programs reject applicants who type less than 25-30 words per minute for secretarial training. A Denver skills center requires secretarial applicants to possess a high school diploma and pass two typing tests before admission.[4]

The subcontractors who provide services to enrollees may perform additional screening. More than half of a sample of service providers in Illinois established entrance criteria, typically involving academic proficiency, in addition to the SDAs' qualifications.[5] Some SDA administrators have reported that service providers screen 20-25 eligible applicants for each training opening. One SDA used a 10-point system designed under CETA to favor individuals with the greatest impediments to sustained employment. However, an administrator noted that the system broke down under JTPA: "Previously lots of sixes and sevens got into the training programs; the contractors just won't take them now. They look for ones and twos." Three-fourths of a sample of SDAs noted that JTPA participants are better educated, have more job experience, and have less need of support services than CETA's clientele. One administrator explained why SDAs accepted service provider screening: "This is the trade-off: we expect high placement rates and low costs; they [service providers] get the freedom to take whoever they think will help them achieve that."[6]

A comparison by the U.S. General Accounting Office of JTPA and CETA client characteristics in a matched sample of 148 CETA prime sponsors and SDAs with identical boundaries showed few differences.[7] National totals of recorded participant characteristics also indicate few differences between the two programs. These findings do not prove that creaming is absent in JTPA, however, because qualified participants who are similar in age, sex and years of schooling may differ widely in employability. While SDAs generally make no effort to define or recruit those most in need of assistance, they usually set recruitment goals for women, minorities and welfare recipients and specify these targets in contracts with service providers. Service providers generally have the discretion to choose the best qualified applicants within these parameters, which may explain why reported client characteristics do not indicate creaming.

Creaming did not originate under JTPA. In fact, one study of CETA found that almost all local prime sponsors used educational criteria to screen out applicants, and that administrators generally accepted the screening practices of service providers.[8] However, several reasons make it likely that creaming is practiced more extensively under JTPA. First, cost and job placement performance standards put pressure on SDAs to select more employable enrollees. Particularly in the case of adult performance standards, which give SDAs credit only for job placements, there is little incentive to invest funds in enrollees requiring remedial education before entering occupational training. Many SDAs pursue a deliberate policy of serving as many individuals as possible at the lowest possible cost per trainee, which inhibits assistance to enrollees requiring more intensive training to enhance employability. Finally, the larger business role in JTPA and the concomitant emphasis on business needs probably also promotes creaming. Employers do what comes naturally and favor the most qualified applicants.

Although JTPA's ostensibly high job placement rates have garnered much praise for the program, the evidence indicates that SDAs deliberately select more qualified applicants and exclude those most in need in order to achieve this result. However, this politically safe policy may be economically inefficient in the long run, since job training programs produce the greatest *net* impact by serving individuals with greater labor market handicaps.[9]

Characteristics

In 1985, Title IIA programs enrolled about 1.1 million participants, nearly identical to the number assisted by the principal CETA training program during the late 1970s. However, in order to maintain this enrollment level, administrators had to cut inflation-adjusted expenditures per enrollee by a third. Even by relying on low cost services, JTPA's appropriation permits assistance to only about one in 20 of the working-age poor.

The typical Title IIA enrollee is an unemployed high school graduate under age 30. Participants are about equally divided between whites and minorities, two-fifths receive public assistance, and a quarter have dropped out of school (table 3.1).

SDA training programs are required by law to allocate 40 percent of total funding to youth enrollees. However, almost half the SDAs have difficulty meeting the youth spending requirement, which they attribute to the shortage of eligible youth in their area, the law's restrictions on stipends which could have been used as an incentive to enroll youth, inadequate recruiting, and an emphasis on low-cost services. The General Accounting Office suggested that a more important factor determining an SDA's inability to meet the youth requirement was the absence of special programs targeted toward 16-21 year olds.[10] Despite these difficulties, the 40 percent youth spending requirement has undoubtedly promoted greater service to youth than would otherwise have occurred. Many policymakers believe that assisting young people will reap a greater net long-term impact than aid to adults, but this assumption rests largely on faith. Emphasis on training assistance to youth has fluctuated significantly over the past quarter century.

Table 3.1.
Characteristics of 1.1 million Title IIA participants (1985).

	Total	Adults	Youth (<22)
Male	48%	47%	49%
Female	52	53	51
White	51	55	46
Black	33	30	37
Hispanic	12	12	13
Under 22	44	-	100
22-54	54	97	-
Over 54	2	3	-
High school dropout	26	27	26
High school student	17	1	37
High school graduate	57	72	37
Public assistance recipient	40	44	36
AFDC recipient	21	22	20
Unemployment insurance claimant	6	10	2
Handicapped	10	8	12
Limited English	4	5	3

Source: U.S. Department of Labor, Employment and Training Administration

Women constitute slightly more than half of JTPA participants. Compared to male enrollees, women are slightly older and better educated, more likely to be black, twice as likely to be receiving cash welfare, and more likely to have been out of work for at least six months at enrollment.

Two of five participants receive public assistance, including some who benefit from more than one program. A third receive food stamps, a fifth are AFDC recipients, and slightly less than a tenth obtain state or local general assistance or refugee assistance. States with higher than average AFDC payments tend to enroll a higher proportion of their welfare rolls in JTPA than states paying less than the national average (29 vs. 20 percent).[11] This may imply that states with higher AFDC payments make greater efforts to enroll recipients in order to reduce welfare costs, or that the enrollees are better qualified for undergoing training. The finding also apparently contradicts the common notion that states with *relatively* high AFDC payments discourage the work ethic.

Administrative Limitations and Support Services

JTPA departed radically from CETA in restricting income and support services to trainees. Federal CETA administrators generally *required* local programs to pay allowances equal to the minimum wage to all classroom trainees, even 14-year-olds in the summer program. Total support expenditures, including classroom training allowances, work experience wages and outlays for other services, accounted for 59 percent of the 1982 CETA training budget.[12] CETA's stipend policy was based on the assumption that the poor could not pursue sustained training without income support. A disadvantage of this policy was that, given the low earnings of CETA's clientele, stipends could present an attractive alternative to work for some trainees.[13]

Taking this speculation as fact, the Reagan administration charged that stipends made CETA an income support rather than a training program, and proposed to ban the payments altogether. After a prolonged and bitter debate, Congress and the administration reached a compromise requiring SDAs to devote at least 70 percent of Title IIA expenditures to training. No more than 15 percent can be spent on administration, and no more than 30 percent on combined administration and support costs (including allowances and supportive services such as transportation assistance and child care). The new rules have almost completely eliminated allowances. Spending in 1985 was reportedly allocated as follows:

Training	75%
Administration	14
Support	11

The law leaves "training" largely undefined, but Labor Department regulations permit direct training costs to include outlays for equipment, classroom space, job-related counseling, and half of the costs for work experience if less than six months duration and combined with another form of training. Other work experience costs are considered a support service expense. Most states classify participant recruitment and eligibility determination costs as training expenditures. Contractor profits are probably also recorded as training expenses, but because separate reporting of profits is not required, it is impossible to estimate such costs.

During JTPA's first three years, the SDAs reported that administrative outlays accounted for 14-15 percent of their Title IIA expenditures. However, neither Congress nor the Labor Department adequately defined administrative expenses, allowing SDAs to fudge management costs and to claim that their programs are lean and trim. Labor Department regulations allow SDAs to hide administrative expenditures by counting *all* performance-based contracting costs as training expenses. Performance-based contracts involve withholding full payment from job trainers until the enrollee finds a job. A large but unreported proportion of SDA funds is allocated through performance-based contracts, significantly understating JTPA's true administrative costs. Even with the loopholes, SDA administrators claim that the cost limits have had a negative impact on local management by constricting staff size as well as monitoring and evaluation activities.[14]

The law directs SDAs to include allowances, half of work experience expenditures, and other assistance necessary to enable participants to remain enrolled in training programs (including transportation, child care and health care) as support service costs. Apparently, program administrators do not find the cost limitations onerous, because few SDAs request waivers. In fact, on the average, SDAs report that they spend only three-quarters of the allowable funds for provision of services; a U.S. General Accounting Office survey found that support spending accounts for only half of the allowable 15 percent.[15] The skimping on support services reinforces the allegations of creaming and the proclivity of SDAs to stress "pure" training. Only one of six participants receives support services. Even if it is assumed that all support costs are for allowances and various support services (i.e., ignoring the work experience costs allocated as support), average support spending in 1985 amounted to only $161 per participant, or about $11.50 a week. Arguing that JTPA's reduced budget should be channeled directly to training and that support assistance encourages dependency, SDA policymakers hold support costs to a minimum. The law notwithstanding, by 1987 the view that support services were outside JTPA's responsibility was widespread. As a North Dakota JTPA official put it, "Those clients who need other social or human services prior to skill training should be served by other programs designed to remove those barriers."[16]

Transportation, child care and medical assistance are the most typical support services offered, the latter usually restricted to job-related needs such as eyeglasses or required physical exams. The SDAs typically deny assistance to on-the-job training or work experience program enrollees on the grounds that they receive wages and therefore should be able to provide for their own needs. The most common means of providing assistance are through direct cash payments to enrollees, set-asides in contracts with service providers, and unfunded agreements with outside agencies. Referral of enrollees to social service agencies, which have faced severe funding losses during the 1980s, does not guarantee that the individuals receive assistance. The 20 percent of JTPA enrollees who receive AFDC are automatically eligible for health assistance through medicaid.

Less than 1 percent of JTPA Title IIA funding is spent on allowances. Only one of seven participants receives stipends, averaging $34 weekly. Payments are based on such factors as the number of hours spent in training, household size, income, and commuting distance to the training site.

Denying support services has had a deleterious impact on JTPA's effectiveness. More than half of SDA administrators and service providers surveyed believe that because of the limits, JTPA enrolls individuals who are less disadvantaged then CETA participants. A majority also believe that they must operate curtailed training programs because enrollees, lacking income support, cannot afford long-term training. One positive impact noted by SDA directors is that participants are more motivated to pursue training and are not in the program to obtain a stipend.[17] However, it could also be argued that the enrolled participants are likely to secure jobs on their own and that provision of basic needs should come before "building character."

As JTPA professionals often note, "You can't eat training." Many poor individuals who require income and support services to initiate and complete a job training program are excluded from JTPA. Congress should consider liberalizing the statutory support service cost limitations, and the Labor Department should encourage SDAs to expand services to participants who need help. To optimize the impact of limited resources, stipends should be adjusted to the income needs of the enrollee's family. In addition, SDAs should husband resources carefully by monitoring participant progress and dismissing enrollees whose main interest appears to be stipends rather than training.

Training

JTPA Title IIA programs offer many occupational courses similar to CETA's, but despite this continuity JTPA's practices differ greatly from its predecessor. Four distinct components account for the bulk of JTPA enrollment. Classroom and on-the-job training averages no more than about three to four months. Job search training, designed to hone participants' job hunting skills, is much shorter, usually lasting two weeks or less. Finally, work experience programs place youth with limited employment backgrounds in entry-level jobs with government agencies and nonprofit organizations. Some JTPA participants receive no assistance other than counseling.

Although the categorization of services in the two programs differs somewhat, the SDAs substantially expanded OJT and job search assistance and reduced work experience and classroom training compared to CETA (figure 3.1). National training distribution data mask an incredible degree of diversity among SDAs. Forty JTPA Title IIA programs exhibited the following differences in the proportion of participants enrolled in different types of services.[18]

Service	Range
Occupational classroom training	2-76%
Basic education	0-20
On-the-job training	3-64
Job search	10-37
Work experience	0-22

The factors that account for different service options are unclear. An examination of CETA training found little connection between local economic conditions, client characteristics, and the type of services offered.[19]

Classroom Training

Most JTPA classroom training is directly job-related, although a small proportion is devoted to remedial education. Relatively more women, blacks, the long-term (over six months) unemployed, and public assistance recipients tend to be assigned to classroom programs.

Classroom training programs are extremely brief, most scheduled for between three and six months, but some for as little as two to six weeks. JTPA trainees typically receive nearly 30 hours of instruction weekly for a little over four months, a month less than the average CETA classroom trainee. The actual difference is undoubtedly even greater than the data indicate, because until 1986, when Labor Department regulations proscribed the practice, SDAs could categorize program completers in a "holding status" for up to three months which some SDAs counted as part of the training courses.

Figure 3.1
Compared to CETA, JTPA substantially expanded on-the-job
training and job search assistance.

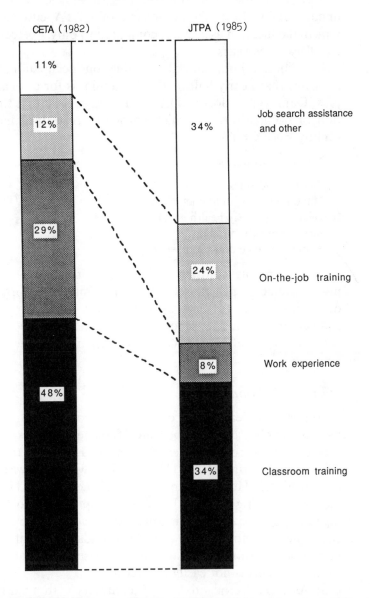

Source: U.S. Department of Labor, Employment and Training Administration

Since many SDAs deny admittance to applicants considered educationally deficient, it follows that JTPA downgraded remedial education compared to the role this training component played under CETA. In 1982, 14 percent of CETA enrollees received remedial education assistance, compared to only 7 percent of JTPA enrollees three years later.

The limited information available on occupational offerings indicates that nearly half of JTPA training is for clerical and sales jobs. Data from a dozen SDAs examined suggest that the distribution of occupations for which enrollees are trained has changed slightly since CETA.[20]

Training occupation	CETA	JTPA
Clerical and sales	38%	43%
Machine trades and benchwork	22	16
Technical (mostly health care)	13	19
Service (mostly building maintenance and food service)	12	10

SDAs typically contract with service providers — most commonly public or private schools, community-based organizations, or businesses — to serve an entire class of JTPA participants. Individual referrals to schools are atypical, usually restricted to cases where an entire class cannot be organized, especially in rural areas.

On-the-Job Training

OJT involves learning an occupational skill through work. SDAs usually reimburse firms for half of the employee's wage costs, theoretically to reimburse employers for additional training costs and to induce firms to hire JTPA eligibles who otherwise might not be considered. However, absent careful monitoring JTPA may in fact be providing windfall benefits to employers who take advantage of the subsidy for individuals they would have hired in any case. The law restricts the use of JTPA funds to "activities which are in addition to those which would otherwise be available," but this vague standard is not easily enforceable.

SDAs typically negotiate OJT contracts with small businesses who train no more than a few enrollees for entry-level jobs. As a rule, SDAs first screen applicants to select those who are likely to be acceptable to the employer, and then refer several applicants to the employer, who makes a final choice. Average OJT training duration is a little less than 3.5 months, about a month shorter than under CETA.[21]

The proportion of enrollment in OJT has doubled since CETA. The local business representatives whose influence increased under JTPA tend to favor OJT, and the program offers significant advantages to SDA administrators working within the constraints of JTPA's performance standards and cost limitations. OJT has always produced high placement results because administrators often require employment commitments beyond the reimbursement period in return for the wage subsidy, and since enrollees receive wages they generally do not need either allowances or support services.

Not surprisingly, employers tend to select the most qualified applicants for OJT slots. In fact, some SDAs even allow employers to recruit their own OJT participants. White men (two-thirds of OJT enrollees), adults, high school graduates, individuals not receiving public assistance, and those unemployed for less than six months are overrepresented in OJT compared with other forms of training. The Labor Department has not yet released data on the earnings of JTPA participants before enrollment, but comparable CETA data indicate that OJT trainees had consistently higher pre-enrollment earnings than other participants. With increasing employer influence and a widespread orientation toward serving the needs of business, the creaming problem is undoubtedly more widespread under JTPA. For example, the Houston PIC announces that its OJT program is designed "for businesses that want to reduce labor costs and increase profits."[22]

Employers participating in CETA perceived only minor differences in productivity between OJT trainees and other employees, which may mean that the firms were taking no greater risk than normal in accepting OJT trainees. Furthermore, without sufficient on-site monitoring there is little indication of how much training OJT enrollees actually receive. Employers who sponsored CETA on-the-job trainees reported devoting little more staff time to orient and instruct OJT trainees than other employees. Firms estimated that under CETA they devoted about 42 hours total staff time to train or orient OJT trainees, or about 2 hours a week.[23] If the same practices continue under JTPA, it seems likely that OJT may function more as a wage subsidy to induce the employer to hire a JTPA-referred worker than as a reimbursement for presumed additional training time required by a JTPA enrollee. Some SDAs acknowledge using OJT in this fashion. However, the experience of CETA as well as the more recent Targeted Jobs Tax Credit demonstrates that absent careful monitoring, many employers hire individuals they would have employed without government inducements, but still collect the subsidies.[24]

Job Search Assistance

At least a fifth of JTPA participants are engaged primarily in brief job search programs. One analyst concluded from examining SDA records that it is difficult to distinguish job search assistance from "other services," and that the former is probably underreported. Enrollees deemed job-ready are placed in job search programs. Studies of JTPA's dislocated worker program indicate that the projects frequently limit enrollment to individuals who have either job leads or actual offers, a practice probably pursued by Title IIA programs as well. The range of job search assistance includes preparing resumes, locating job openings, direct referrals to employers, interviewing tips, and job clubs providing advice and support. Project participants usually receive several days of instruction before pursuing a self-directed job search with some advice and material assistance (typewriters, phones, copying machines, etc.) from SDAs. National reporting data indicate that the average job search participant is enrolled for four weeks, but these figures undoubtedly include a holding period during which enrollees receive no assistance. A study that examined local SDA operations found that job search programs typically last no more than two weeks.[25]

Year-Round Youth Programs

In 1985, nearly half a million youths below age 22 were enrolled in Title IIA. The majority of youth enrollees receive classroom, on-the-job, and job search training, although they constitute a minority within these programs (figure 3.2). In contrast, most participants in work experience and miscellaneous training programs are under 22. SDAs place most work experience enrollees in part-time jobs in a variety of government agencies and nonprofit organizations. Seventy percent of youth work experience enrollees are in high school. National data, which most likely exaggerate program duration, indicate that the average enrollee remains in a work experience program for 4.5 months. Work experience programs last longer than other forms of JTPA training, although since most enrollees are students they probably work less than 20 hours a week.

Because nearly two- fifths of youth enrollees are in school, the law specifies that positive outcomes of youth programs must include school completion, military enlistment, and — most significantly — successful completion of a "competency-based" program. Such programs typically tutor enrollees in basic education, job-specific skills, "world of work" awareness or job search techniques, and probably account for much of the assistance categorized as "miscellaneous" services.

Figure 3.2
**Most enrollees in work experience and miscellaneous training
programs are under age 22 (1985).**

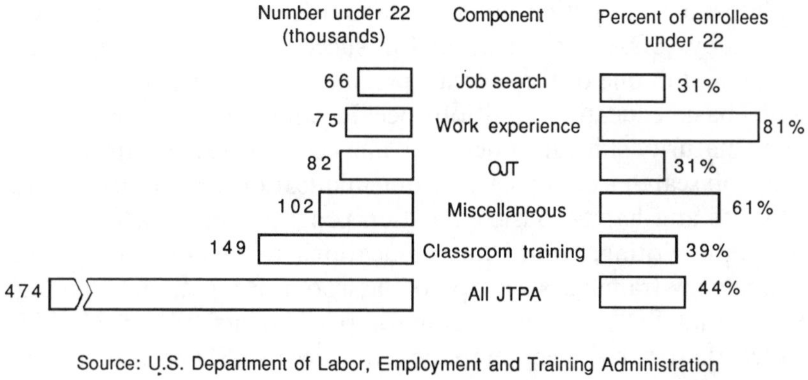

Number under 22 (thousands)	Component	Percent of enrollees under 22
66	Job search	31%
75	Work experience	81%
82	OJT	31%
102	Miscellaneous	61%
149	Classroom training	39%
474	All JTPA	44%

Source: U.S. Department of Labor, Employment and Training Administration

Source: U.S. Department of Labor, Employment and Training Administration

Despite congressional emphasis, JTPA competency-based programs have gotten off to an extremely slow start, although appropriate models were readily available.[26] Ignoring the law, the Labor Department's initial positive termination standards gave SDAs no credit for providing youth with basic competencies. The department reversed its decision after JTPA got underway, but did not define what SDAs could count as a competency-based outcome until June 1986. In the intervening two-and-a-half years the states were responsible for ensuring that SDA competency-based programs were "sufficiently developed," but less than half the states attempted to enforce this vague standard.

The law is ambiguous about who is responsible for determining acceptable competency standards. In somewhat confusing language, JTPA states that the Labor Department shall prescribe performance standards, including attainment of "employment competencies recognized by the private industry council." Many state and local officials have interpreted this provision as delegating complete approval authority over employment competencies to the PICs, and not surprisingly the Office of Management and Budget agrees. The House-Senate conference report on JTPA makes it clear, however, that both the Labor Department and the states were intended to supervise competency-based standards.

The Labor Department has not been helpful in resolving the confusion. It issued guidelines governing acceptable competency-based programs, but focused primarily on process issues rather than on substance, rejecting content standards as infringing on local autonomy. SDAs are credited for successful youth competency attainment in one of three areas: preemployment or work maturity skills, basic education, and job-specific skills. Preemployment and work maturity skills include labor market knowledge, career planning, job search techniques, consumer education, and positive work attitudes and habits. Basic education programs may include reading, math, writing, or oral communications instruction. Job-specific competency training is similar to classroom occupational training, except that SDAs receive credit for participants' enhanced skills rather than subsequent employment success. SDAs are free to operate any of these three types of competency-based programs or none at all, although it is nearly impossible for SDAs to meet the

Labor Department's positive termination performance standards without operating at least some competency programs.

The U.S. General Accounting Office reported that only about three-fifths of the SDAs it surveyed operated competency programs in 1985. The most commonly offered programs were in the least rigorous preemployment and work maturity skills area, and only a quarter of the SDAs operated basic education projects and a quarter operated job skills projects.[27] More recent Labor Department data indicate that about four of five SDAs now operate competency programs, although emphasis on education and job skill competency programs probably remains limited. The Office of Management and Budget has repeatedly blocked Labor Department efforts to collect the information necessary to evaluate SDA competency programs.

Summer Youth Programs

In addition to Title IIA youth training, JTPA's Title IIB continues a summer jobs program for youth first initiated as a component of President Johnson's antipoverty efforts and a stable fixture of federal employment programs ever since. The projects typically pay 14-to 21-year-olds the minimum wage for part-time work in government agencies and community-based organizations. The summer program constitutes a major part of JTPA, with an annual price tag of about $750 million. However, the Labor Department did not collect even basic data on enrollees until 1986, precluding a credible assessment. The department did finance an evaluation of the CETA summer program before the transition to JTPA.[28] Because the current program is similar except for increased provision of remedial education, the study's findings as well as other relevant CETA data probably fairly represent the JTPA summer program.

Other summer programs for disadvantaged youth complement JTPA's Title IIB. The Targeted Jobs Tax Credit program provides a tax break for employers who hire poor 16- and 17-year-olds during the summer. The special summer credit is more generous than the year-round TJTC program. Employers can receive a tax credit of 85 percent of up to $3000 paid to eligible youths during the summer. However, the effective maximum tax break of $2,550 is somewhat less than this, depending upon the specific tax liabilities of the employer. Despite the generous terms, credits were issued for only 27,000 teenagers in 1985. There is probably little coordination between JTPA's and TJTC's summer programs.[29]

Several states and localities operate summer youth corps programs which provide minimum wage jobs primarily on public land, involving work on conservation and maintenance projects. Total state and local funding is less than $20 million. The Michigan Youth Corps, which spends $15 million to provide 12,500 jobs, is by far the largest of the state programs.[30]

Financing and administration. Annual JTPA appropriations for summer youth jobs (in millions) have fluctuated widely:

1984	$824.5
1985	824.5
1986	724.5
1987	636.0
1988	750.0

Adjusted for inflation, funding for 1988 is only about three-quarters of the average CETA appropriation during the 1979-81 period. While overall funding is lower, the uncertainty formerly associated with appropriations has undoubtedly diminished under JTPA because of the new forward funding system. Due to last minute congressional wrangling over CETA summer jobs spending, local prime sponsors sometimes received funding after operations began, precluding project planning. The Reagan administration has repeatedly attempted to limit funding for the summer program, but Congress has rejected these proposals except for 1987. In January 1987 the President proposed an $800 million budget and offered amendments allowing SDAs to serve young AFDC recipients year-round with Title IIB funds.

The allocation of summer program funds is based primarily on adult unemployment rates, using the same formula applicable to year-round training programs. Consequently, urban areas with a high proportion of poor youth are underfunded. Because of the costs entailed, it is impractical to ascertain annually the distribution of poor youths among the SDAs. However, decennial census data suggest that the regional distribution of poor youth is nearly identical to the distribution of poor 16-65-year-olds. Thus using poverty rather than unemployment data may mitigate funding fluctuations and inequities in the summer program.[31]

The summer jobs program is administered by state and local officials and private industry councils in the same manner as the Title IIA program. Congress specifically exempted the summer program from the cost limits applied to other JTPA programs, but Labor Department regulations prohibit summer programs from spending more than 15 percent of total costs on administration. Reported administrative spending was slightly lower.

During the late 1970s, the U.S. General Accounting Office found that many youths were not adequately supervised on the job and were therefore probably not receiving useful work experience. Consequently, the Labor Department monitored summer programs more closely and required local administrators to increase their oversight activities. Analysts found no serious problems at work-sites visited in 1983, and concluded that enrollees received mean-ingful employment experiences. Following JTPA's enactment, fed-eral monitoring has been pro forma at best, and there is little indication that the states exercise careful oversight of SDA summer programs.

Typically, one worksite employee supervises five enrollees, al-though the ratio ranges from 1:1 for technical jobs to 1:10-12 for maintenance or conservation crews. Supervisors include both reg-ular worksite employees as well as temporary summer program employees who lead the work crews. Orientation assistance varies from brief sessions to two days of formal training, although most programs provide manuals to supervisors. Because the orientation is usually held at central locations, not all supervisors can leave work to attend. Supervisors almost unanimously endorse the summer program as a worthwhile endeavor, but offer several criticisms. Many believe they need more training on how to manage teenagers. Few programs make adequate efforts to match enrollees' job assignments with their interests, which produces frustration for all parties. Finally, supervisors recommend that programs dismiss participants with excessive absences to maintain the morale of other enrollees, and institute a rewards system for exemplary youth.[32]

Enrollees and services. Eligibility for participation is based on the same income criteria as Title IIA, but 14- and 15-year-olds also qualify for Title IIB. Of the approximately 5-6 million eligible youth, about 750,000 or 12-15 percent enroll each summer. Local recruitment efforts often generate more applicants than can be placed in jobs. Administrators use a variety of techniques to address this dilemma, including lotteries, first-come first-served enrollment policies, point systems which favor targeted groups, and restrictions on the number of hours participants can work in order to spread available funds.

The typical summer youth enrollee is a minority high school student (table 3.2). Compared to youth in Title IIA programs, summer enrollees are younger (a third are 14- or 15-years-old), less likely to be white or dropouts, and more likely to be AFDC recipients. JTPA and CETA summer enrollee characteristics differ little.

Table 3.2
Nearly two of three Title IIB enrollees are
minority high school students.

	CETA (1981)	JTPA (1986)
Total	766,400	743,700
Male	52%	51%
Female	48	49
14-15	35	34
16-19	59	40 (16-17)
20-21	6	26 (18-21)
Dropout	6	6
High school student	82	81
High school graduate	13	13
White	33	32
Black	50	43
Hispanic	14	20
AFDC recipient	37	NA
Single parent	3	3
Handicapped	7	11
Limited English	4	10

Source: U.S. Department of Labor, Employment and Training Administration

Although the law permits SDAs to provide a wide variety of services to summer youth enrollees, the program has remained primarily a work experience program with some remedial education and "world of work" instruction. Participants usually work 32 hours per week for six to eight weeks at the federal minimum $3.35 hourly wage.

Most enrollees work at government agencies, schools and community-based organizations. The summer program's lengthy history allows administrators to establish long-term relationships with agencies and offices which previously provided satisfactory work opportunities. Moreover, widespread budget cuts have stimulated demand for subsidized summer enrollees. Program administrators can afford to be choosy in selecting worksites.

Most participants are assigned to maintenance, clerical or office work positions, but other assignments include aide positions in agencies serving the elderly, handicapped and children; making car deliveries; and working on conservation projects. In one locale, youth helped record the oral histories of Indochinese immigrants; in another, enrollees worked at a cable TV studio and were able to participate in filmmaking. However, given the age and inexperience of most enrollees, such assignments are atypical.

Summer programs typically provide enrollees with a total of two to three days of "world of work" instruction, including an explanation of the labor market and various occupational opportunities, job search and interview tips, and help with preparing resumes. Some administrators conduct group seminars, while other programs delegate world of work training to worksite supervisors. The quality of instruction varies greatly, but reports from both administrators and enrollees indicate that these programs are generally inadequate and uninteresting to the youth.

In 1982, only 3 percent of total summer participants received occupational training. Whether participants are assigned to work experience or training positions, few receive job placement help and even fewer obtain unsubsidized jobs which might enable them to work part-time during the school year.[33]

In 1986 the summer program devoted an average of 5 percent of its budget to provide basic education to about one in ten enrollees, an investment similar to the 1982 CETA program.[34] Following 1986 congressional amendments requiring SDAs to assess the reading and math skills of enrollees, and to spend at least some money on basic education, the SDAs planned to increase their provision of remedial assistance as follows:

	1986	1987 (estimate)
SDAs providing basic education	57%	100%
Title IIB funds devoted to education	5	12
Enrollees receiving assistance	8	21

Most SDAs rely on reading and math tests to determine enrollees' need for remediation. However, nearly a third of local projects restrict remediation enrollment to students only, excluding drop-outs — who may need help the most — and graduates. Education participants receive an average of 12 hours instruction weekly (at a cost of $775), and spend another 20 hours at their work experience assignment. Projects commonly offer enrollees stipends or academic credit to encourage class attendance, and some make work experience job offers contingent upon enrollment in remedial courses. Few SDAs provide basic education themselves; most rely on local schools.[35]

An assessment. Assessing the impact of summer employment programs is difficult both because of a paucity of data and disagreements over the appropriate goals of the program. During the riot-torn summers of the 1960s, the program was commonly referred to as "fire insurance" because it helped keep teenagers off the streets. The current program places more emphasis on educational goals.

Research on the program's impact has focused on evaluating the benefits of summer work experience alone or in combination with remedial education, and determining to what extent localities use the summer jobs for government activities which would have been performed in any case. Work experience has produced tangible benefits for communities as well as providing enrollees with both job opportunities and income. However, numerous studies demonstrate that summer work experience by itself does little to improve future employability and earnings, for which more intensive skills training is necessary.[36]

A six-year experimental program supplementing summer work experience with remedial education is now in progress. The project provides 14-15- year-olds likely to drop out of school with 90 hours of basic reading and math instruction as well as a short course aimed at reducing teen pregnancy. Results from the project's first two years are encouraging. Poor, deficiently educated youngsters, who typically experience learning losses during the summer, maintained their reading level and slightly increased their math proficiency. Enrollees bettered the control group's performance by half a grade in reading and nearly a full grade in math. These results represented an improvement over the first year's outcomes, largely because a standardized curriculum replaced the previous practice of allowing each school to develop its own program. Sexually active participants were 50 percent more likely than the control group to use contraceptives — nearly half of both groups were sexually active at the beginning of the summer. Instructional costs per enrollee amounted to slightly more than $500, in addition to the costs of about $1000 per participant for the average summer program.[37]

In 1983 some localities used summer youth enrollees as substitutes for regular government employees, thereby effectively substituting federal for local funds.[38] However, given the age and inexperience of the participants, it is unlikely that the substitution problem was very serious.

Summer work experience programs have provided jobs to millions of poor youth who probably would not otherwise have found work. This role is extremely important, especially in the case of minority youth with disturbingly low labor force participation rates and even lower employment to population ratios. However, several changes could enhance the program's effectiveness. First, the available funds could be spread further by paying less than the minimum wage to 14- and 15-year-olds. Second, the Labor Department should encourage SDAs to increase basic education offerings. Nearly a third of the SDAs believe that summer remedial education is the responsibility of the school system and not JTPA. Congress may need to reconsider 1986 proposals requiring SDAs to devote a specified proportion of Title IIB funds to remediation in order to prod these laggards. Third, the Labor Department should develop curriculum standards for brief job search courses which would teach enrollees to prepare resumes, locate openings and interview for job opportunities. Finally, a portion of summer program funds should be reallocated to Title IIA youth training or education programs. Despite the increase in short-term costs, investments in education and training will reap more lasting gains than work experience programs.

Miscellaneous Training Issues

Little is known about the quality of JTPA training. The federal government has failed to monitor training quality, and private industry councils generally rely upon reported placement and cost outcomes rather than reviewing curricula and visiting training sites.[39] A U.S. General Accounting Office study shortly before CETA's demise found that programs which carefully considered program assignments, provided assistance appropriate to participant needs, and carefully monitored training progress had much higher placement rates than other prime sponsors. However, administrators often routed applicants to available openings, paying scant attention to participant needs, and neglected to contact participants following enrollment to smooth obstacles to successful program completion and subsequent employment.[40] While no similar assessment has been made since 1982, it is unlikely that the situation has improved.

The proportion of enrollees receiving sequential training — e.g., remedial education followed by OJT or classroom occupational training — is not known, but the number cannot be very large. Two-fifths of the SDAs enroll participants in a single program only.[41] Under the Labor Department's reporting system, participants receiving sequential training are placed in the "other services" category, accounting for 11 percent of enrollees. Average reported training duration for these individuals is only a little over three months, allowing little opportunity for sequential training, and the "other services" category includes many participants who are in school or only receive job search assistance.

Congress directed the SDAs to increase training opportunities for women in nontraditional occupations, but local programs have largely ignored this directive and occupational training remains highly sex-segregated. A Wisconsin study found that women were primarily trained to be waitresses, secretaries, hospital attendants, cashiers and tellers, while men prepared for work as janitors, cooks or kitchen helpers, truck drivers, and for various construction positions. Congress also encouraged SDAs to boost service to displaced homemakers, typically middle-aged women with little employment experience who are entering the labor market due to divorce or the death of their spouses. However, very few programs actively recruit displaced homemakers, and those SDAs which do so provide these women primarily with job search assistance, which can hardly be expected to supply them with employable skills.[42]

Service Providers

SDAs utilize many training institutions which operated under CETA. However, the relative importance of various training contractors and the assistance they provide have changed significantly. Most SDAs use more than one agency to recruit and select enrollees, and SDAs typically subcontract training instead of operating programs directly. Only one of six SDAs provided all training directly in 1985, and about two-thirds subcontracted at least half their training funds (figure 3.3). The most widely used subcontractors are public education institutions, operating in 85 percent of the SDAs. Postsecondary schools are the most commonly utilized education institution, although about half the SDAs contract with public high schools.[43]

Thirty percent of the SDAs use for-profit schools to provide primarily job-specific training, but the training is generally expensive, which clashes with JTPA's emphasis on reducing costs, and the schools tend to vigorously screen applicants. For example, one proprietary school turned down 25 JTPA eligibles for every 1 accepted, and another screened 118 eligible individuals to enroll 19.[44] Further reflecting the role that business representatives play in determining JTPA policy, two-thirds of the SDAs turn to private employers to offer on-the-job training, although some of the SDAs which decided to rely heavily on OJT have encountered difficulty in developing enough training positions.

Figure 3.3
Most SDAs subcontract training.

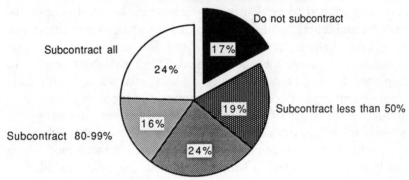

Source: National Alliance of Business

Community-based organizations (CBOs), nonprofit groups which provide a variety of services to the needy, played an increasingly important role in employment and training programs during the 1960s and 1970s. Major CBOs with nationwide networks include Opportunities Industrialization Centers of America, Inc., SER-Jobs for Progress, the AFL-CIO's Human Resources Development Institute, 70001 Training and Employment Institute, the Urban League, and Wider Opportunities for Women. The role of CBOs has diminished considerably under JTPA. For example, two of the larger CBOs experienced the following reductions from their height under CETA to JTPA.

	Opportunities Industrialization Centers	SER-Jobs for Progress
CETA		
Local affiliates	148	65
Funding (millions)	$150	$119
JTPA (1987)		
Local affiliates	80	40
Funding (millions)	$ 49	$ 35

Although about 80 percent of SDAs contract with at least one CBO, only half of these utilize CBOs for any training. The others use CBOs for outreach, eligibility determinations, or helping JTPA terminees find jobs. In most of the local programs which have no contracts with CBOs, no CBOs operate within the SDA's boundaries.[45]

The major reason for the decline of CBOs under JTPA was the elimination of CETA public jobs and Youth Employment and Demonstration Projects Act programs in which CBOs played an integral role. JTPA's severe restrictions on work experience programs and allowance payments and emphasis on performance standards also severely hurt CBOs. The rise of performance-based contracts, with full payment delayed until terminees find work, has caused cash flow problems for CBOs dependent upon JTPA funds for survival.[46] The poor quality of training offered by many CBOs may also have played a role in their exclusion as providers of training. However, CBOs are important for recruiting individuals most in need and representing the interest of the needy.[47] The declining role of CBOs reflects JTPA's emphasis on the needs of business rather than the needs of the individuals JTPA was designed to help. Altogether, a third of the CBOs operating CETA programs were not awarded SDA contracts, but most of these did not even apply for funding because their role was curtailed under JTPA.[48]

In addition to recruiting and training enrollees, subcontractors also help find jobs for many JTPA terminees. Program operators are often expected to place their own enrollees, but almost two-thirds of SDAs use a variety of institutions to place JTPA graduates.[49]

Entity used for job placement	SDAs using entity
Training provider	53%
SDA administrative agency	43
Employment service	30
Community-based organization	20
Public school	18

In line with JTPA's emphasis on low costs, short-term training and high job placement rates, contractors who fail to meet these specifications are weeded out. One former CETA contractor noted that in order to obtain a JTPA contract, his agency had to switch from "taking the tough cases to becoming an efficient personnel office for local businesses." Illinois youth service providers who had operated under CETA indicated that they reoriented their JTPA programs away from remedial and vocational training toward preemployment and job search assistance.[50]

Performance-based contracting rapidly emerged following JTPA's enactment and has provided several distinct advantages to SDA administrators. Contractors have a powerful incentive to place their trainees — or to report them as placed — which helps the SDA to claim success in achieving the performance targets. Second, performance-based contracting permits "management by numbers," minimizing on-site monitoring time and expense. Finally, Labor Department regulations allow SDAs to categorize administrative and support services expenditures as "training" costs if provided through performance-based contracts. As noted, this enables SDAs to evade the law's strict nontraining cost limitations. By 1985, performance-based contracts accounted for three of four SDA contracts with service providers. The contracts typically specify uniform job placement and cost targets regardless of enrollee characteristics, giving contractors every incentive to select the most qualified individuals.[51]

Despite their popularity, SDAs have noted two disadvantages to performance-based contracting. The absence of advance funding can present serious problems for contractors dependent upon JTPA financing. Second, such arrangements encourage contractors to overstate placements to claim the maximum possible profit, and therefore require careful monitoring, which is not widely practiced under JTPA. A Massachusetts PIC director, in characterizing the consequences of JTPA's so-called performance-driven system, noted, "The move towards performance-based contracts has raised the specter of programs designed and operated for the numbers game."[52] Performance-based contracts can represent a useful tool for holding service providers to their commitments. However, JTPA's experience demonstrates the importance of augmenting performance-based contracts with standards for training quality, follow-up monitoring, and measures to prevent creaming.

4

Performance Standards
and Results

Perhaps the most important factor which led Congress to emphasize performance standards was widespread, though largely unsubstantiated, criticism of the Comprehensive Employment and Training Act. As dissatisfaction with CETA mounted, Congress directed the Labor Department in 1978 to develop performance standards to assess the effectiveness of the program. Four years elapsed before the Labor Department implemented performance criteria on a trial basis, but the experiment was abandoned during the transition from CETA to JTPA.[1] Performance standards appealed to JTPA's designers as a way to eliminate the need for detailed, costly oversight by the federal government, so long as localities delivered results.

The use of objective, measurable and fair standards to judge the quality of job training programs is universally hailed but not easily accomplished. Legislative pronouncements typically represent declarations of vague intent rather than realistic objectives. Consequently, administrators must specify performance measures and the means of achieving them. Key outcomes such as a "quality job" and "educational achievement" require definition, taking into account the abilities of the program's clientele. Equally difficult is the task of adjusting standards for localities with radically different economic conditions, client characteristics, and training institutions. Even many quantifiable factors elude precise measurement, and performance standards are no better than their statistical foundation. For example, local unemployment statistics are little better than guesstimates.[2] Even under the best-designed system, significant factors that affect performance, such as participant motivation, are difficult to measure and are thus ignored.

Poorly drafted performance standards may produce the appearance of program success without the substance and also cause unintended and deleterious side-effects. Guidelines which reward operators for graduating enrollees from educational programs but fail to specify the educational standards can produce the "successful" attainment of meaningless credentials which may well be disregarded in the market place. Even when the standards are carefully defined, the administrators may respond by selecting the most qualified applicants, undermining the goal of helping those who most need assistance. Granting their obvious potential usefulness, performance standards nevertheless cannot fully answer the question, "How much difference does JTPA really make?" Carefully designed experiments which randomly assign individuals with similar characteristics to training and control groups may provide insights, but such efforts are costly and frequently difficult to implement in more than a handful of local programs.

JTPA's Requirements

Congress decreed that "the basic return on [JTPA's] investment is to be measured by the increased employment and earnings of participants and the reductions in welfare dependency." The law directs the Secretary of Labor to prescribe adult performance standards which *may* include placement in unsubsidized jobs, job retention, increases in earnings, and reduced welfare payments. For youth, the following criteria *must* also be considered: attainment of competency-based standards, successful completion of school or an equivalency degree program, and enrollment in other training programs or the military. The standards must consider participants' labor market experience both before enrolling and after program completion. Finally, the law requires the establishment of cost standards applicable to the above measures. The Labor Department may modify the performance measures no more than once every two years.

Apart from the difficulties inherent in designing and implementing performance standards, the law presents two major problems.

First, JTPA's drafters confused performance standards with impact evaluations, which attempt to gauge the *net* impact of a program. For example, the law emphasizes decreased welfare dependency and the postprogram employment and income status of recipients following their training. About half of all recipients leave the welfare rolls within two years, most without any additional government assistance (although many later return). Thus many recipients who participate in JTPA would probably have left the welfare rolls without job training. Determining the net impact of JTPA would require tracking an appropriate control group of welfare recipients who did not enroll in JTPA. Performance standards are unsuited to determining the program's net impact, because they only measure results without gauging JTPA's contribution to the outcome. After a false start, the Labor Department did not begin impact assessments until 1986, and the project's implementation has been fraught with difficulties.

The second problem presented by the law is the application of performance standards to competency-based programs devoted to teaching enrollees basic education, training them for entry level skills, or exposing them to job search techniques. Applying performance criteria to such disparate activities requires standardized program guidelines and detailed information for each program component, which few if any SDAs maintain. Moreover, standardized federal program regulations clash with JTPA's emphasis on state and local control.

Despite these statutory flaws, the inclusion of performance standards in the law represents an advance. But this achievement has been partly vitiated by the Labor Department's overreliance on performance standards to the exclusion of other means of overseeing JTPA, and the overemphasis SDAs placed on the targets. In addition, the administration's implementation of the standards themselves has been deficient in a number of important respects.

Federal Implementation

The Labor Department's choice of seven performance standards (four for adult enrollees and three for youth participants) was based on both the law and the criteria considered during the CETA years.

National Performance Standards (1986-7)

Adult

Entered employment rate (total)	62%
Entered employment rate (welfare recipients)	51%
Hourly wage	$4.91
Cost per placement	$4,374

Youth (16-21)

Entered employment rate	43%
Positive termination rate	75%
Cost per positive termination	$4,900

The entered employment rate standards are defined as the proportion of JTPA terminees who find jobs. The two cost standards reflect total outlays divided by the number of job placements (plus other positive outcomes for youths). The seven standards have remained in effect since 1983, but the numerical targets for each standard have, in most cases, been made more stringent.

The positive termination standards applied to youth are ambiguous. These benchmarks are supposed to measure the proportion of 16-21-year-olds who obtain work; successfully complete a competency-based program; return to school after dropping out; complete primary, secondary or postsecondary schooling; or enroll in other training programs or the military. The Labor Department, however, left the definition of youth competencies up to localities, and the U.S. General Accounting Office found that programs range from rigorous classroom training to one-session motivational seminars. These extreme variations preclude meaningful comparisons between SDAs using the positive termination standards, and in fact discourage quality programs by giving equal credit to brief, superficial courses.[3]

In devising the performance standards, the Office of Management and Budget and the Labor Department initially flouted the law's requirement that trainees' postprogram experiences be considered. Both the job placement and hourly wage standards are based on the JTPA trainee's first day on the job. No distinction whatsoever is made between temporary or permanent employment, or part-time or full-time jobs. The Office of Management and Budget refused until 1986 to allow the Labor Department to even collect data to establish postprogram standards. This has effectively delayed post-program measures until at least mid-1988, six years after JTPA's enactment.

Setting proper target figures for placement rates, earnings, and costs necessarily reflects tentative judgments. Information about the normal labor market experiences of the poor and the impact of training is at best fragmentary, and performance targets conse-quently reflect the values and best estimates of administrators. The Labor Department initially used 1982 CETA performance results as a baseline, then arbitrarily adjusted the figures upward. The depart-ment raised most of the standards by 10 percent, for example, because of an undefined "productivity improvement factor" that by the stroke of a pen made JTPA more efficient than CETA.

The law also requires the Labor Department to devise adjust-ments to the performance standards to produce equitable measures for SDAs facing varying economic conditions and enrollees. Four of five states currently use the Labor Department's optional adjustment methodology, and it has a significant impact on the performance standards. In states which use the department's model, SDA performance is judged by adjusted standards which may differ greatly from the national standards.

One important reason for the discrepancy between the adjusted standards and the national standards is that until 1986 the Labor Department issued two sets of performance standards annually: the national standards and model standards (table 4.1). The depart-ment holds that the law's prohibition on changing the performance standards more frequently than biennially does not apply to the model's performance standards. For example, although the na-tional standards remained unchanged between 1984 and 1985, the department made the targets relatively more difficult to attain by significantly tightening the adjustment model's performance stan-dards. Despite this action, most SDAs were still easily able to meet — or at least claim to meet — the standards. In 1986, for the first time, the national standards and the model's standards were identical for five of the seven benchmarks.

Table 4.1
The actual performance standards SDAs faced often differed drastically from the national standards.

Performance standards	National standards (1984-5)	Model standards (1984)	Median adjusted standards (1984)	Model standards (1985)	Median adjusted standards (1985)	Range (1985)	National standards (1986-7)	Model standards (1986-7)
Adults								
Entered employment rate (total)	55%	47%	57%	57%	56%	31-71%	62%	62%
Entered employment rate (welfare recipients)	39%	None	48%	None	48%	4-97%	51%	51%
Hourly wage	$4.91	$4.44	$4.63	$4.64	$4.63	$3.13-6.74	$4.91	$4.64
Cost per placement	$5704	$6242	$4167	$3740	$4570	$2185-9153	$4374	$4374
Youth								
Entered employment rate	41%	21%	34%	36%	35%	12-57%	43%	43%
Positive termination rate	82%	80%	75%	75%	76%	61-98%	75%	75%
Cost per positive termination	$4900	$2710	$3453	$3362	$3557	$496-6002	$4900	$3711

Source: U.S. Department of Labor, Employment and Training Administration

The second important element of the adjustment model is the various economic, demographic, and client characteristic factors used to adjust the standards. The annual adjustments are based on the correlation between these factors and past performance results, and a regression methodology is used to estimate the relative importance of each factor. CETA data were used until JTPA information became available in mid-1985. The local unemployment rate, average wage, proportion of families in poverty, and population density are the components for determining the different economic conditions that prevail in SDAs. Adjustments for varying participant characteristics include the proportion of enrollees who are welfare recipients, high school dropouts, handicapped, members of various minority groups, females, and students. The only training factor considered is the duration of training measured in weeks. The same factors are not used in adjusting each of the seven performance standards, and factors have been added or dropped from one year to another to attempt to improve the model's predictive ability. For example, the population density factor was added in 1986 for four of the performance measures.

The 1986 adjustments to the adult job placement standard for Cleveland illustrate the model's application to a high unemployment area where the SDA serves a severely disadvantaged population. The performance standard is derived by applying the Labor Department "weights" to the difference between Cleveland's demographic and economic characteristics and the average for all SDAs. With these adjustments, Cleveland's adult job placement standard is reduced to 47 percent, well below the national standard of 62 percent (table 4.2).

An examination of the 1984 and 1985 adjusted standards shows the significant variations between the national and SDAs' median adjusted performance standards (table 4.1). In some instances the basis for the discrepancies is puzzling. That the adjusted adult job placement standard was slightly higher than the corresponding national standard seems reasonable, since the model incorporated the 1982 recession level unemployment rate, and it is likely that job placements rose during the recovery when unemployment dropped. However, the adjusted youth job placement standard was much lower than the corresponding national standard.

The adjusted cost standards for adults and youth were significantly lower — more difficult to meet — than the national standards. The adjusted job placement standard for welfare recipients
was also more stringent than the national standard. In contrast, the
adjusted adult wage standard and the youth positive termination
standard were both more lenient than the respective national
standards.

The adjustment factors had a much greater overall impact on the
model standards in 1984 than in 1985. In the latter year, there was
very little difference between the model and the median adjusted
standards, except for the adult cost placement benchmark. However, in 1984 the adjustment factors effectively tightened the model
standards in all cases but the youth positive termination rate. Some
of the principal adjustment factors responsible for these shifts raise
serious concerns about the validity of the Labor Department's
model. The Labor Department's highly questionable assumption
that it would be *less* costly for the SDAs to serve single mothers
made the adult cost standard much more difficult to meet. For
youth, the principal reason for the divergence between the median
adjusted standards and the model standards for all three benchmarks was that the SDAs served a higher proportion of high school
graduates. However, it is unclear why serving more graduates
should simultaneously make placements more difficult to achieve
and positive terminations (which include job placements) easier.

To ensure that the performance standards would be uniformly
applied across the country, the Labor Department in 1983 proposed
mandatory adoption of the adjustment methodology. However, the
Office of Management and Budget rejected this proposal on the
grounds that it would unduly interfere with state autonomy.
Consequently, state use of the department model is optional.
Governors can either apply the national performance standards
directly to the SDAs, or adjust the standards utilizing their own or
the Labor Department's methodology. Labor Department regulations require that state-developed adjustment methodologies be
based on reliable data and applied consistently among SDAs. The
states are free to make different adjustments for each of the seven
standards. A state may apply the national standards to the job

Table 4.2
The Labor Department's adjustment model greatly reduces Cleveland's adult entered employment standard.*

Adjustment factors	Cleveland	-	Average for all SDAs	=	Difference	X	DOL weights	=	Adjustment
Economic and demographic factors									
1. Population density(thousands of persons per square mile)	3.27		0.6		2.67		.827		2.21
2. Unemployment rate	12.7		8.0		4.7		-.717		-3.37
3. Average annual wage (thousands of dollars)	20.4		16.9		3.5		-.653		-2.29
4. Proportion of poor families	9.1		9.4		-0.3		-.223		.07
Participant characteristics (percentages of all terminees)									
5. Welfare recipients	61.6		29.8		31.8		-.252		-8.01
6. Dropouts	35.1		25.0		10.1		-.172		-1.72
7. Handicapped	4.1		9.1		-5.0		-.128		.64
8. Blacks	73.0		23.8		49.2		-.073		-3.59
9. Females	46.5		52.8		-6.3		-.063		.40
					Total				-15.66
					Model standard				62.40
					Adjusted standard				46.74

*Only the most significant factors in the model are listed, using Cleveland's 1985 data.

placement target, the Labor Department-adjusted standard to the wage benchmark, and a state-adjusted standard to the cost criteria. Three states have rejected the Labor Department's model and at least six states have considered such a move. If more states follow suit, the uniformity of the national performance criteria would be undermined. Nationwide consistency was further impaired by the Labor Department's decision to allow SDAs to use either the 1986 or the 1987 adjustment model in calculating their 1987 performance standards.

The adjustment factors are designed to compensate for the problems of SDAs which face relatively severe economic conditions or serve a disproportionately disadvantaged clientele. Conversely, the adjustments also attempt to discourage SDAs from trying to beat the system by enrolling more qualified applicants. However, the adjustment factors alone cannot prevent creaming, and important flaws render the claimed scientific validity of the Labor Department's model questionable.

First, the formula can only be as reliable as the data or the standards upon which it is based. However, the economic and demographic data given the most weight are unreliable or outdated. As indicated previously, local unemployment data are little better than guesses. Poverty adjustments are based on 1979 data. While population density data may remain relatively stable in the short run, they are a questionable measure of the accessibility and cost of transportation to the poor. The inaccuracy of the estimates is further compounded by the fact that geographic boundaries for the data reported by the Census Bureau and other agencies do not necessarily coincide with the geographical jurisdictions of the SDAs. Information on participant characteristics, if properly collected and reported, is more accurate, but these factors generally have less influence on the adjustment model. Training duration figures are extremely deficient both because of poor collection procedures and because duration is defined as weeks rather than hours of training.

Apart from these general deficiencies, other difficulties afflict specific standards. Because the youth positive termination rate and the cost per positive termination are poorly defined, the adjustments have little meaning. In the case of the job placement standard for welfare recipients, the Labor Department's technical consultants have concluded that the adjustment model does not satisfactorily explain the range of performance among SDAs.[4]

The Labor Department's inconsistent application of the adjustments over the 1984-87 period also raises doubts about the validity of the models. For example, four local economic and demographic factors strongly influence the adult job placement standard, but only the local unemployment rate is used to modify the youth placement benchmark. Educational attainment is not considered in the adult cost standard adjustment, although it is more costly to train educationally deficient participants. The weights for many of the factors have changed greatly from year to year, and occasionally the department changes the *directional* value of a given factor — that is, factors which would make the standard harder to meet one year have been changed to make the target easier to attain in the next. Some of the Labor Department's modifications represent reasonable adaptations to changing conditions or corrections of past misjudgments, but the changes have been too extensive to inspire confidence in the overall method. For example, the proportion of enrolled unemployment insurance recipients was considered one of the most important factors in adjusting the job placement standard in 1984, but by 1986 its influence in the model was almost negligible. The same is true for the proportion of enrolled older workers, a factor not even included in the 1987 model.

State Direction

Although the federal role in performance standards is supposed to be preeminent, governors have the authority to mandate additional performance criteria, modify the federal standards, award monetary incentives to SDAs which exceed performance standards, and sanction SDAs which perform poorly. Federal nonintervention further augments state flexibility in implementing performance standards.

To date, however, the states have wielded little of this authority, even to address widely acknowledged program deficiencies. JTPA requires SDAs to serve those "most in need," and to allocate "equitable services" to welfare recipients and school dropouts. However, both the Labor Department and the states have generally failed to enforce these requirements, in spite of numerous reports that SDAs ignored these provisions. The states also accord a low priority to promoting effective youth competency standards.[5] With regard to postprogram measures, the majority of states collected posttraining data before the Labor Department issued regulations on the subject in 1986, but virtually all failed to implement standards measuring job retention.[6]

Providing financial awards to SDAs which exceed performance standards and sanctioning SDAs which perform poorly was supposed to provide governors an important means of exercising influence over local operations, but the SDAs deny that the incentive grants exert much influence on local policy.[7] Six percent of a state's Title IIA funds, a little over $100 million nationally, is annually allocated to governors for incentive awards and for technical assistance. However, during JTPA's first three years, the states spent only a third of the available 6 percent set-aside funds. Of the funds spent, the states devoted about half to incentive awards rewarding exemplary performance. The law also requires governors to provide incentives for SDAs which target "hard-to-serve" individuals, but the states allocate only about a tenth of their 6 percent funds toward this goal. The remaining 40 percent of the set-aside is used for technical assistance.[8]

If an SDA fails to meet performance standards for two consecutive years, the governor must intervene and choose a new administrative entity, restructure the PIC, select different service providers, or take other action necessary to improve performance. Technical assistance must be offered before the governor steps in. While precise information is not available, the National Governors' Association has no record of a single case where a state sanctioned an SDA for failure to meet performance standards.

Governors may modify the national performance standards by using either the Labor Department's adjustment methodology or their own model. However, even states which use the federal methodology can make additional adjustments for local conditions, and nearly half the states do so but to a very limited degree. States granted adjustment requests to less than 100 SDAs, most commonly for the adult wage or youth job placement standards in cases where the SDA's unemployment rate or client characteristics deviated substantially from the national averages.[9] Recognizing the imprecision of the model, the Labor Department also allows governors to adjust performance standards within a predetermined "tolerance range," but few states do so. Tolerance range adjustments for 1986 were as follows:

Adults	**Range (+/-)**
Entered employment rate (total)	3.7 percent
Entered employment rate	
(welfare recipients)	3.8 percent
Hourly wage	$0.13
Cost per placement	$450
Youth	
Entered employment rate	5.2 percent
Positive termination rate	5.0 percent
Cost per positive termination	$400

Standards and Reality

SDAs reported that they met all four performance standards for adults but did not do as well for youths. In 1985, seven of every ten adults found jobs paying an average hourly wage rate of nearly $5 at a cost of about $3000 per placement. Job placements exceeded the standards at a lower cost than allowed by the standards, and the average hourly wage rate was exactly on the mark (table 4.3). However, the national positive termination rate for youth was well short of the designated target until 1985.

Table 4.3
SDAs were generally able to exceed the performance standards.

	Standards Results (Oct.1983–June1984)		Standards (1984-5)	Results (1984)	Results (1985)
Adult					
Entered employment rate (total)	58%	66%	55%	67%	69%
Entered employment rate					
(welfare recipients)	41%	55%	39%	57%	57%
Hourly wage	$4.90	$4.82	$4.91	$4.85	$4.91
Cost per placement	$5,900	$3,308	$5,704	$3,395	$2,941
Youth					
Entered employment rate	41%	54%	41%	52%	50%
Positive termination rate	82%	73%	82%	74%	78%
Cost per positive termination	$4,900	$2,817	$4,900	$2,561	$2,317

Source: U.S. Department of Labor, Employment and Training Administration

JTPA's claimed results significantly exceed CETA's performance except for hourly wages. CETA placement rates ranged from 39-48 percent over 1978-82 (compared to 60 percent for all 1985 JTPA terminees), and CETA's average cost per placement was over twice as high as JTPA's. However, JTPA adult and youth terminees earned about 10 percent less than CETA participants after adjusting for either inflation or average wage growth, even though CETA served a slightly higher proportion of youth, as follows:

	Average hourly wages
JTPA (1985)	$4.65
CETA (1981)	
Actual wages	4.32
Adjusted for inflation	5.27
Adjusted for wage growth	5.18

Placement and wage rates are strongly correlated with both demographic characteristics and the type of training received (table 4.4). Placement rate differences between men and women are neither large nor consistent across different types of training. However, male enrollees have significantly higher wages: in fact, male high school dropouts earn on average more than women with a high school diploma but no further education. However, gender earnings differentials are not as great as for the total labor force, probably because JTPA trainees qualify mostly for entry-level occupations. Placement rates for whites average 10 percentage points higher than blacks, while Hispanic performance is midway between the two groups; differences in wage rates exhibit a similar pattern.

Public assistance recipients, the long-term (over six months) unemployed, and high school dropouts find job less often than the average enrollee, although the reported placement rates for dropouts is a surprisingly high 59 percent. Wage rates are the mirror image of placement rates for these three groups, with dropouts more likely to obtain a job but with the lowest average wage.

Not surprisingly, on-the-job trainees are much more likely to obtain work with relatively higher wages than most other trainees, since the most qualified applicants are assigned to OJT and most continue to work for the same employer (figure 4.1). Selective

Table 4.4
JTPA Performance (1985).

Characteristics	Total		Classroom Training		On-the-job Training		Job Search		Work Experience		Other Services	
	Placement rate	Hourly wage	Placement rate	Hourly wage	Placement rate	Hourly wage	Placement rate	Hourly wage	Placement rate	Hourly wage	Placement rate	Hourly wage
Total	62%	$4.65	54%	$4.80	76%	$4.81	75%	$4.53	42%	$4.04	51%	$4.40
Adults	70	4.92	59	5.02	79	4.98	77	4.78	63	4.70	70	4.82
Youth	51	4.15	48	4.37	70	4.37	71	3.95	37	3.78	40	3.92
Male	63	4.92	54	5.12	74	5.15	78	4.75	38	4.20	54	4.56
Female	61	4.39	55	4.60	78	4.40	71	4.26	45	3.93	50	4.22
White	66	4.73	59	4.84	79	4.91	77	4.68	47	4.08	57	4.47
Black	55	4.43	49	4.63	70	4.50	71	4.33	38	3.89	42	4.24
Hispanic	61	4.63	51	4.92	75	4.61	77	4.43	30	4.09	49	4.41
Public assistance recipient	57	4.48	49	4.64	74	4.53	68	4.38	37	3.93	50	4.39
Dropout	59	4.37	45	4.49	76	4.50	71	4.18	51	4.30	55	4.19
Unemployed six months prior to application	54	4.56	48	4.70	72	4.66	70	4.54	36	3.98	41	4.33

Source: U.S. Department of Labor, Employment and Training Administration

Note: National totals differ slightly from those presented in table 4.3 because data in this table are based on a sample of enrollees.

enrollment practices also probably contribute to job search terminees' high placement rates. Classroom trainees (some of whom
receive only remedial education) have relatively low placement rates
but they receive the same hourly wage rates as OJT participants and
25 cents per hour above job search graduates. Those assigned to
either work experience programs or miscellaneous "other services"
have both low placement and wage rates, largely because many of
these enrollees are high school students.

Figure 4.1
Placement rates and earnings differ markedly by type of training.

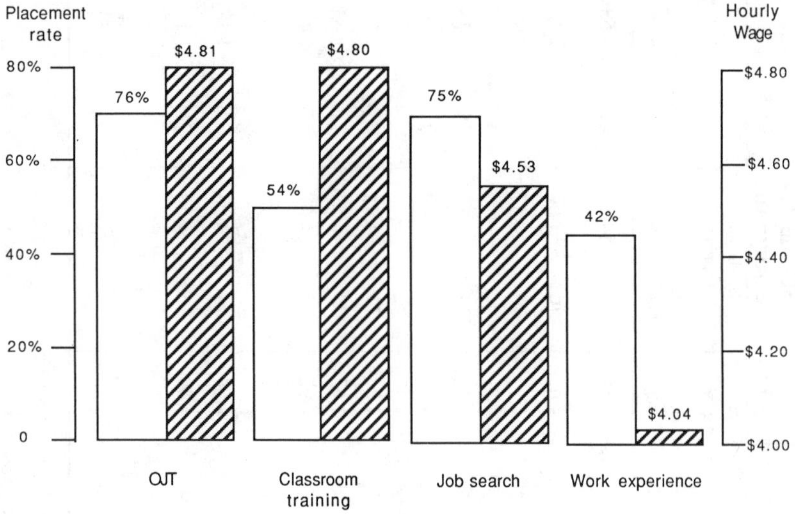

Source: U.S. Department of Labor, Employment and Training Administration

Not all observers believe that JTPA's results demonstrate unqualified success. There are good reasons to believe that the program's
reported performance is exaggerated, and administrators' single-
minded focus on producing good numbers has promoted creaming
and discouraged more intensive training.

Selected state postprogram surveys show that roughly a third of
the trainees employed at termination are out of work three months
later. However, in Massachusetts, with nearly full employment, 90
percent of employed terminees retained their jobs. In several states
where follow-up results are recorded for individuals not employed
at termination, between 30 and 50 percent find work within three

months. Almost all of the employed adults work full time. Former OJT trainees are the most likely to retain their jobs, followed by classroom training graduates. Retention rates for other terminees are generally significantly lower, but this is probably attributable to the high proportion of youths in the other programs.[10]

Widespread anecdotal reports indicate that many SDAs and service providers manipulate enrollment and termination reporting to inflate placement rates. In Illinois, one-fourth of the service providers examined did not officially enroll individuals until training was underway to avoid counting early program dropouts who were less likely to find work. Some service providers waited until a likely job was identified, and one agency delayed all paperwork and only submitted the names of individuals who were almost certain to complete the program.[11] Program termination reports are similarly manipulated to enhance claimed results. As already indicated, many SDAs place graduates in a three-month "holding status," reporting the placement rate not at termination but instead within the following three months. A Michigan SDA places graduates in nonpaying "internships" until they obtain employment to avoid counting them as jobless. State and SDA definitions of acceptable job placements vary widely. Denver considers a trainee placed if the employer confirms that the hiring decision has been made, while in another SDA the individual must remain employed for over five months to count as an acceptable placement.[12]

Instances of outright fraud are not unknown. A Washington, D.C. contractor receiving half a million dollars reported that almost all graduates found jobs, while in reality almost none had.[13] While such incidents are probably rare, the SDAs' inattention to monitoring clearly leaves JTPA vulnerable to flagrant abuses. A 1982 U.S. General Accounting Office examination of 35 randomly selected proprietary schools found that half the schools inflated their job placement rates beyond what their own records indicated. In addition, employers contacted had not hired individuals the schools claimed to have placed with them in one of five cases.[14] Absent careful monitoring, there is good reason to believe that reporting is even more suspect under JTPA, as reimbursement is often contingent upon placement success. Follow-up surveys in two states indicate that claimed placement rates may be exaggerated by 5-10 percent.[15]

Pressure to meet the original performance standards and maintain high performance led to widespread creaming. Many local administrators who acknowledge creaming argue that federal policy leaves them little alternative. This "devil made me do it" alibi is somewhat disingenuous because rather than protesting against performance standards, most SDAs trumpet their figures as proof of local program success. Nevertheless, both the law and federal policy supply a strong impetus toward creaming. Without allowances, it is impossible to train the individuals lacking independent means of support who probably need help the most. Federal adult cost standards, reduced by a third since JTPA's inception after adjusting for inflation, hinder SDAs from providing the deficiently educated the basic competency and training they need to secure better jobs. However, the average adult cost per placement for 1985 was $1600 below the median adjusted standard, demonstrating the SDAs' eagerness to provide even less intensive assistance than the performance standards allowed. Enforcement of the law's mandate to serve those "most in need" could provide some counterweight against creaming, but would entail increased costs per placement.

In enacting JTPA, Congress recognized that a performance standards system had potential drawbacks. The law directs the National Commission for Employment Policy, a JTPA-funded federal advisory group on employment issues, to evaluate the impact of the Labor Department's standards. The commission funded a descriptive study of state performance standard policy, but it has only recently begun to take the necessary steps to determine the impact of the standards on participants, services and costs as required by law.

Finally, the evolution of training under JTPA raises serious questions about program quality. The proportion of on-the-job and job search training increased from about a fifth to nearly half of all training from CETA to JTPA. Cost limitations, superficial performance standards and business influence had more to do with this shift than the track records of OJT and job search in improving future employability. JTPA's emphasis on job search assistance is in some ways beneficial because few individuals are knowledgeable job hunters. However, the SDAs' failure to combine job search with more intensive training is troubling. Virtually every study of job search assistance has concluded that while the training has clear short-term benefits, the impact dissipates within one to two years. On the other hand, the congressional decision to limit work experience programs was probably justified except for welfare recipients, because careful research has indicated that this is the only group that benefits from work experience.[16]

In contrast to other forms of assistance, quality classroom training has a proven track record for cost-effectively improving enrollees' long-term job prospects. Comparisons for JTPA are not available, but during CETA, classroom trainees had proportionately higher long-term earnings gains than participants in other forms of training.[17] Classroom training remains the most popular service offered by SDAs, but the proportion of participants trained in the classroom has declined from almost half under CETA to a third under JTPA. Moreover, average classroom training duration has dropped by a month since CETA, although the Labor Department recognizes that longer and more comprehensive training is crucial in improving enrollees' employability.[18] A study of CETA found that graduates' subsequent earnings increased more than proportionately with lengthier training.[19] Research on the Job Corps program for poor youths yields identical findings.

Does Training Work?

Most CETA and JTPA research indicates that the programs improve the skills, earnings, and employment rates of participants. Studies of CETA found that enrollees' higher earnings were primarily due to increased working time rather than higher hourly wages. Also, the positive impact was apparently not directly tied to occupationally-specific training because, with the exception of those trained for clerical jobs, within two years most CETA terminees no longer worked in their field of training.[20]

There is less agreement regarding the relative merits of classroom and on-the-job training in enhancing employability. Most CETA evaluations were based on comparing the experiences of CETA participants with a very different "comparison" group derived from a sample of the Current Population Survey.[21] In attempting to equitably compare the experiences of two such different groups, researchers made statistical adjustments to control for divergent earnings histories and demographic characteristics. The inherent weakness of this method is demonstrated by the fact that, although each study used essentially the same data, researchers often arrived at startlingly different conclusions.[22]

The Labor Department's follow-up of enrollees in 20 SDAs to evaluate JTPA will not be available before 1990. Few states or SDAs have critically assessed their operations. An Indiana study which is better than most found that former enrollees made considerable gains in the two years following program participation. Although the comparison group was clearly more advantaged than the JTPA participants, the earnings of white female and black male former enrollees actually surpassed those of the comparison group.[23] Vermont found that employed adult terminees boosted their hourly wages by an average of 14 percent over their previous jobs. Most enrollees with job experience viewed their new job as a step up from prior positions.[24]

In sum, while JTPA probably improves participants' employability, its achievements fall far short of the Labor Department's claims made on its behalf. Although the introduction of performance standards — if appropriately implemented — should have improved the quality of training, JTPA's single-minded focus on attaining dubious numerical targets may have done more harm than good. As a Lima, Ohio administrator explained, "We must show paper success whether clients are served or not."[25] In its review of CETA shortly before JTPA's enactment, the U.S. General Accounting Office concluded that "relying solely on placement rates to monitor program performance is inadvisable."[26] Disregarding this advice, the Reagan administration heavily emphasized placement-based performance indicators and neglected other means of monitoring JTPA. Responsibility was delegated to the states, few of whom provided constructive leadership.

5
Aiding
Dislocated Workers

The dynamics of economic change have invariably led to the obsolescence of occupational skills and the displacement of workers. The anxieties of displaced workers that new jobs will not become available have been exaggerated, as economic growth has usually been accompanied by rising productivity, generating new jobs and better working conditions. The economic and psychological adjustments faced by displaced workers are nonetheless formidable.

In the early 1980s, several factors combined to produce grave economic dislocation in the United States, as an ever increasing number of industrial as well as newly developing nations became fully competitive with American industry in world markets. According to one estimate, trade difficulties resulted in a net loss of about two million jobs between 1979 and 1984.[1]

The transition of employment from the goods-producing to the services sector in recent decades was compounded by the onset of the worst recession since the Great Depression. Ironically, even the prolonged economic recovery following the 1981-2 recession did not end the dislocation problem because other nations pursued vigorous export policies, taking advantage of the overvalued dollar and the reinvigorated purchasing power of Americans. The U.S. Bureau of Labor Statistics estimated that more workers were displaced in 1985 than in any previous year in the 1980s.

To aid dislocated workers, Congress added a new component to federal job training legislation. However, when Congress enacted JTPA's Title III dislocated worker program, it possessed little reliable information about the magnitude and nature of the dislocated worker problem. The Congressional Budget Office estimated shortly before JTPA's passage in 1982 that the number of dislocated workers ranged between 100,000 and 2.1 million, depending on the definition of the term.[2] Dislocation had not been considered a serious problem since the early 1960s, and it literally took an act of Congress to compel the Reagan administration to survey the extent of worker dislocation. However, the survey's preliminary results were only available two years after JTPA's enactment.

Assessing the scope of dislocation is compounded by the difficulty of defining who is a dislocated worker and determining the labor market impacts of dislocation. To estimate the number of displaced workers, the Bureau of Labor Statistics decided to include workers who had held their previous job for three years or more and were laid off due to the shutdown or relocation of a plant or company, slack work, or the abolition of their position. The BLS definition is narrower than that favored by some observers who argue for the inclusion of previously self-employed job losers and against the exclusion of those with less than three years tenure. On the other hand, the BLS definition is more expansive than alternatives which count only job losers from declining industries. Definitional disagreements reflect differing viewpoints about the reemployment difficulties experienced by job losers. Some analysts believe that dislocated workers with lengthier job tenure face greater readjustment problems, particularly if they are displaced from declining industries, than other job losers. However, the evidence on whether dislocated workers face longer unemployment spells or greater subsequent wage losses than other job losers is not conclusive.

Dislocated workers constitute about 10-20 percent of the unemployed. The latest Bureau of Labor Statistics survey found that 10.8 million workers aged 20 years and over were dislocated between 1981 and 1985, including 5.1 million with at least three years tenure. Sixty-seven percent of the latter were employed in January 1986, 18 percent were unemployed, and 15 percent had dropped out of the labor force. Forty-four percent of the workers who regained full-time employment earned less than in their previous job. Minority, unskilled, deficiently educated, and older workers suffered disproportionately severe reemployment problems.[3] An analysis of a 1984 BLS survey found that nearly half of the reemployed dislocated workers had changed occupations. Operators, fabricators, and laborers moving into service occupations accounted for most of the shift.[4] Most jobs in these broad occupational categories require few skills.

Programs Antedating JTPA

Concerned about the impact of automation on unemployment, Congress enacted in 1962 the Manpower Development and Training Act (MDTA), the first targeted federal assistance program for dislocated workers. However, when unemployment declined shortly after MDTA's passage, Congress redirected the program toward serving the low-income unemployed.

Also in 1962, Congress enacted what would later become a major and sustained federal effort to aid dislocated workers. The Trade Adjustment Assistance (TAA) program differs from MDTA, CETA and JTPA in that it specifically benefits workers displaced by foreign trade, provides primarily income support rather than retraining, and also assists the affected firms. At its height in 1980, TAA provided more than $1.6 billion to over 500,000 displaced workers. However, the program's high costs and the fact that most beneficiaries were concentrated in a few high-wage industries made TAA an easy mark for budget cutters after 1981. The Reagan administration favored the termination of the trade program, but Congress extended TAA until 1991. In 1987 the program provided income support or job-related assistance to some 60,000 dislocated workers at an estimated cost of $206 million.

To qualify for TAA assistance, the Labor Department must certify that workers lost their jobs as a result of import competition, a judgment that is necessarily not only subjective but also often highly politicized. Job losers employed by a certified firm for at least six months and who participate in a job search program are eligible for a year of benefits. Those enrolled in approved job training programs may receive payments for an additional six months. In fiscal 1987 an estimated 55,000 workers received $176 million in income support, averaging $3200 per person. In addition, qualified individuals are also eligible for state-approved training, job search allowances, and relocation assistance. However, job-related assistance is limited by the available funds. Congress budgeted only $29.9 million for these programs for fiscal 1987, and due to inadequate federal reporting requirements, it is not clear whether states in the past have even fully expended the federal appropriation. Consequently, very few dislocated workers have benefitted from TAA job-related assistance. During 1986, an estimated 7700 persons were trained, 1400 received job search allowances, and 1100 were provided relocation assistance.[5] In 1987 the Reagan administration proposed replacing TAA and JTPA's dislocated worker program with a new program that would more than double total federal aid to dislocated workers and emphasize job-related assistance rather than income support.

JTPA Operations

The Reagan administration's initial opposition to incorporating a new program for dislocated workers as part of JTPA received scant congressional consideration because of rising concerns over dislocation in the midst of the worst slump since the Great Depression. The JTPA legislative debate centered on the larger Title II program, with little attention paid to the dislocated worker program. The staff director for the Senate Employment and Productivity subcommittee characterized the law's language as "remarkably close to the first draft."[6]

Because so little was known about the most cost-effective means of assisting dislocated workers, Congress placed few stipulations on the program, delegating administrative responsibility largely to the states. Both eligibility requirements and authorized services are broadly defined. The most significant restriction is the law's requirement limiting nontraining costs to 30 percent of the federal allocation. In addition, although the law does not prohibit the use of dislocated worker funds for public service employment, Labor Department regulations forbid the practice.

Financing

For 1987, Congress appropriated $200 million for the dislocated worker program (figure 5.1). The law requires that at least 75 percent of the funds be allocated directly to the states. In the absence of regular surveys on dislocated workers in each state, the distribution formula is based on the state's relative proportion of unemployed persons and the relative proportion of individuals unemployed 15 weeks or longer, although the duration of unemployment may not be a reliable indicator of dislocation.

Figure 5.1
States have spent only two-thirds of available dislocated worker funds.

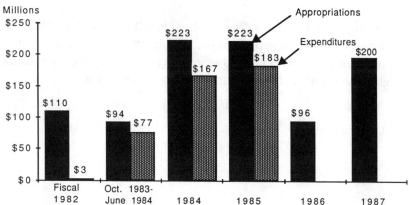

Source: U.S. Department of Labor, Employment and Training Administration

The Labor Department has reserved 25 percent of the dislocated worker appropriation — the maximum allowable under the law — to aid areas facing high unemployment, mass layoffs, or natural disasters. In screening state applications for the funds, the Labor Department considers whether the needs of the area can be met with allocated JTPA or other funds, and also the number of displaced individuals requiring assistance.

Similar to the Title IIA distribution formula, reliance on volatile unemployment rates produces substantial year to year fluctuations in the distribution of dislocated worker funds among the states. However, because the average state spent only two-thirds of its available Title III funds through June 1986, volatile funding allocations probably did not cause serious problems in the states that failed to spend the available funds.

Based on the Bureau of Labor Statistics survey of dislocated workers, the West and Midwest are overfunded while the South gets less than its fair share, if the funds were distributed solely on the basis of total dislocated workers in each region.[7]

Region	Dislocated workers (1981-5)	Title III funds (1982-6)
South	34.1%	27.7%
Midwest	29.9	32.7
Northeast	18.7	19.1
West	17.3	20.5

Ironically, although the South gets less than its fair share of dislocated worker appropriations, the region spends relatively little of its formula funds. The Midwest, which is overfunded, spends the highest share of its formula appropriation, as follows:

Region	Proportion of formula funds spent (1982-6)
U.S. average	70%
Midwest	79
West	70
South	65
Northeast	62

State underspending is primarily attributable to a heavy reliance on low-cost job search assistance and an inability to rapidly organize projects. Eleven states exacerbated their underspending problems by reserving up to a fourth of their federal allocation for contingencies. Because states spent only about half of Title III appropriations through mid-1985, the Reagan administration successfully convinced Congress to reduce 1986 funding by over half, to less than $100 million. The administration argued that unexpended funds carried over from the previous year would allow the states to maintain an even level of funding for dislocated workers. While this was true for the entire country, almost half the states could not maintain equivalent expenditure levels in 1986 because they had spent a relatively high proportion of their previous allocations.[8] Therefore, the budget reduction effectively penalized states which had diligently utilized Title III funds. Congress restored 1987 dislocated worker funding to $200 million.

The Labor Department contends that underspending could be ameliorated by eliminating the allocation formula and providing the department with discretionary authority to distribute *all* Title III funds.[9] However, state officials note that it is impossible to obtain a discretionary grant in less than four months, although one purpose of the fund is to rapidly respond to emergencies.[10] During 1985, the department issued only three grants within the first three-and-a-half months of the program year, two-thirds of the funds were awarded during the last half of the year, and about two-fifths were not issued until the final month. In 1986, according to departmental press releases, a tenth of the discretionary funds were not released until the final week of the program year.

To augment assistance to dislocated workers, the law requires states to match federal funds allocated by formula on a dollar-for-dollar basis. The matching requirement is reduced by 10 percentage points for each 1 percent that the state's unemployment rate exceeds the national average. For example, if the national jobless rate is 7 percent and a state's is 8 percent, the state need only match 90 percent of the federal allocation. A state with a 17 percent unemployment rate would not have to provide any matching funds.

The matching requirement has had a negligible impact on boosting funds for dislocated workers. In 1985, nine states provided only $15 million in matching funds against the $167 million federal formula allocation.[11] The law and regulations are loosely drawn and permit counting in-kind contributions and half of unemployment insurance payments to enrollees in lieu of direct cash contributions. Labor Department regulations which explicitly delegate to governors the responsibility for determining what constitutes an allowable match make the law's requirement even less meaningful. States typically pass the responsibility for generating the phantom matching funds to administrators of local dislocated worker projects.[12] Most local project administrators interviewed by the U.S. General Accounting Office acknowledged that the in-kind resources would have been generated even without the requirement.

The matching requirement has had an impact on the selection of participants and service providers. Both states and localities target services to unemployment insurance recipients, at the expense of other dislocated workers not receiving financial assistance. States also tend to favor service providers such as community colleges who, because of high overhead costs, can easily supply the spurious required match.[13]

Administration

Like JTPA's Title IIA, the dislocated worker program limits administrative and support costs to 30 percent of the federal allocation. The law specifies no further limitation, but Labor Department regulations restrict administrative expenditures to 15 percent. These restrictions only apply to federal formula funds, not to the discretionary allocations. In 1985, projects allocated 79 percent of total dislocated worker outlays to training, 16 percent to administration and 5 percent to support services. Although administrative costs slightly exceeded the limit, it is unlikely that states ignored the regulations because the data include both formula and discretionary fund expenditures. The Labor Department did not require separate reporting for these two categories until 1986.

Although the states possess considerable authority, few display vigorous leadership in administering dislocated worker programs. In addition to their failure to spend the available funds, one study noted that state administrators could not readily name all the dislocated worker projects in their state, let alone provide basic information on project activities.[14]

In 43 states, the same agency administers both the Title II and III programs. The states utilize one of three arrangements for distributing dislocated worker funds: 26 states allocate funds for specific projects, 14 states operate statewide programs through the employment service or community college system, and the balance of the states allocate the funds to SDAs or other political jurisdictions.

The states exercise little oversight of dislocated worker projects. Minimal technical assistance is provided, and state JTPA officials usually do not seek financial or in-kind contributions from companies responsible for layoffs.[15] Most projects collect only federally required information, and a survey of 20 states indicated that only one in four collect follow-up data on participants.[16] The U.S. Office of Technology Assessment criticized the Title III data collection system as "a slender basis for analyzing the performance of JTPA programs, for determining funding needs in relation to performance, for learning from experience, and for improving future performance."[17]

Dislocated Worker Projects

During 1985, 221,000 individuals were enrolled in over 500 Title III projects, a small fraction of the potentially eligible population. A third of the projects are located in New York, California, and Ohio. Each serves an average of 78 enrollees at one time, but the average is skewed upward by about 5 percent of the projects, which serve over 800 enrollees. About two-fifths of the projects are designed for a particular plant, company or industry, but these projects tend to serve other eligible individuals in the surrounding area. Most projects are administered by public institutions, primarily JTPA Title IIA service delivery areas, community colleges and employment offices:[18]

Service delivery areas	31%
Educational institutions	26
Community-based organizations	13
Employment service	9
Unions and/or employers	9
Other state agencies	4
Administrator undetermined	8

SDAs which administer both Title II and III operations usually integrate applicant intake, participant assessments, and job placement efforts for both programs. However, in areas where the SDA does not administer a Title III project — the more common situation — there is little coordination between the two programs.[19] Statutory provisions in the trade adjustment assistance legislation seriously impede coordination with JTPA's dislocated worker program. For example, the law prohibits the supplementation of TAA training funds with money from other federal programs.[20]

Enrollees

Congress opted for a broad eligibility definition for Title III programs, authorizing each state to "establish procedures to identify substantial groups of eligible individuals." States may qualify persons who:

(1) have lost their jobs or received notice, are eligible for unemployment insurance or have exhausted their benefits, and are unlikely to return to their previous industry or occupation;

(2) have lost their job or received notice as a result of a permanent plant closure;

(3) are unemployed for extended periods with limited opportunity for reemployment in a similar occupation in the local labor market; or

(4) were self-employed and are unemployed as a result of general economic conditions in the community.

Using the U.S. Bureau of Labor Statistics definition, but including workers with less than three years job tenure, 3.1 million workers were displaced during 1985, but only 221,000 were enrolled in program year 1985, including 147,000 newly enrolled.

About two of three enrollees are 22-44-year-old white males with high school educations who had previously worked in a manufacturing job. Nearly half are members of low-income households (table 5.1). The Labor Department contends that "the States are conducting sufficient outreach to contact older and less-educated dislocated workers." In fact, high school dropouts and older individuals, who face disproportionate reemployment difficulties, are underserved by dislocated worker projects. A third of unemployed dislocated workers, but only a fifth of enrollees, failed to complete a high school education. A fifth of unemployed dislocated workers, but less than a tenth of the participants, is over 54. The U.S. General Accounting Office found that about a quarter of the dislocated worker projects do not enroll older workers — possibly in violation of JTPA's civil rights provisions — and one of nine excludes individuals with less than a high school education.[21] On the other hand, the long-term unemployed are overrepresented in dislocated worker projects. A third of the enrollees had been jobless more than six months, although only a quarter of the unemployed dislocated workers had been out of work that long.

Table 5.1.
The typical Title III enrollee is a high school
educated white male (1985).

Male	62%
Female	38
White	70
Black	19
Hispanic	8
American Indians, Asians, etc.	3
16-21	4
22-44	73
45-54	14
55 and over	8
Less than high school education	20
High school graduate	80
Receiving AFDC	4
Receiving unemployment insurance	54
Low income	46
Previously employed in manufacturing industry	60

Sources: U.S. Department of Labor and General Accounting Office

Participant characteristic data indicate that the deliberate selection of more qualified applicants, referred to in the trade as "creaming," is common. Case studies of 15 dislocated worker projects, while not representative of all projects — 10 were selected on the basis of their successful job placement performance — provide insights on the participant selection process. Project administrators used a trial job search period lasting from one to ten days as a screening device, and at the end of the period selectively enrolled individuals who had either job leads or offers. Questionnaires and interviews were also commonly used to assess the motivation, however defined, and employability of applicants. Requiring applicants to attend a number of intake events before being formally enrolled was another means to weed out the unmotivated. The projects which emphasized high placement rates practiced aggressive recruitment strategies to enroll more qualified individuals.[22] The U.S. General Accounting Office found that employers selected applicants in 10 percent of Title III projects.[23]

Despite the fact that JTPA serves only a small proportion of dislocated workers, project administrators report difficulty in recruiting enrollees, probably because displaced workers are not aware of the Title III program or in some cases because the projects have poor reputations. Because most projects are ad hoc, short-term efforts, it is impossible to establish a continuous referral network in the community.

Training and Support Services

Labor Department planners originally assumed that enrollees would be retrained for new careers, but local project operators instead emphasize short-term assistance costing an average of a little over $800 per participant. Two-thirds of enrollees receive job search assistance, primarily brief workshops and counseling, but less than half obtain any kind of occupational training or remedial education (table 5.2). However, as is true for Title IIA programs, dislocated worker projects vary markedly in the services they provide. According to the Labor Department, the median length of stay in Title III is 3.8 months, but General Accounting Office reports suggest that this figure is exaggerated.[24]

Job search assistance predominates because of its low cost, short duration (typically two weeks or less), administrative convenience, and a preference on the part of many enrollees for immediate placement rather than training. Based on a sample of 15 projects, the cost per placement for job search programs was only a third as much as either classroom or on-the-job training. Job search programs can be taught in-house to large groups, lowering unit costs. Specialized personnel are not required, and the need for support services is minimal compared with more intensive forms of training. Job search assistance can serve a variety of functions, such as weeding out the unmotivated or separating job-ready participants from those requiring more specialized training.

Table 5.2.
Less than half of Title III enrollees receive any job training (1985).

	Percent of projects offering service*	Percent of partcipants receiving service*	Median duration (weeks)	Cost per participant
Total	-	-	16	$ 828
Job search assistance	84	66	NA	NA
Training	94	NA	NA	NA
Classroom	88	26	9	$2200
On-the-job	67	16	15	$1600
Remedial	32	6	2	NA
Support services	58	23	NA	$ 196
Relocation assistance	14	2	NA	$ 600

Sources: U.S. General Accounting Office and Department of Labor

*Due to multiple responses or participants receiving multiple services, totals are greater than 100 percent.

Where training is offered, it is typically provided in conjunction with job search assistance. Case studies show that a battery of basic education, interest, and aptitude tests are used to screen classroom training participants. The tests tend to be rigorous when the service provider operates under a performance-based contract. According to project administrators, the tests often serve to weed out referrals to vocational schools. In addition to the use of tests, administrators seldom assign participants lacking independent means of financial support to training programs.[25]

Most dislocated worker projects are arranged hurriedly because employers frequently fail to provide advance notice of layoffs. Due to these pressures, limited funding and the fact that most projects last no more than a year, administrators tend to rely upon existing service providers, usually community colleges or vocational schools. Title III projects tend to enroll participants in existing courses rather than working with the institutions to develop courses designed to meet the special needs of JTPA's clientele. Dislocated worker classroom training programs only last nine weeks on average, even briefer than corresponding Title IIA classes. A third of them are 5 weeks or less, and only a fifth last beyond 20 weeks.

About one of six dislocated worker enrollees receives on-the-job training. Title III OJT programs are similar to employer-provided training in Title IIA, and are limited due to the inability of program administrators to procure sufficient OJT slots. The following broad occupational categories are most common in projects providing classroom or on-the-job training:

Occupation	Percent of projects offering	
	Classroom training	OJT
Clerical or office	60%	64%
Semiskilled equipment or machine operation	55	83
Technical paraprofessions	52	42
Skilled crafts or trades	48	60
Service	33	55
Sales	17	41

Remedial education accounts for only 6 percent of total enrollment, despite widespread indications that many enrollees need such assistance. Two-thirds of the projects provide no remedial education.[26] Even where it is available, most projects do not orient remedial education toward dropouts but instead offer two week brush-up classes in conjunction with classroom or on-the-job training. Because of the preponderance of high school graduates in Title III and the availability of remediation classes in local schools, most state officials see no need for additional remedial education assistance from JTPA.[27] Many dislocated workers shun remedial training as a tacit acknowledgment of illiteracy. Sensitive to this problem, some projects design refresher courses specifically for their participants. However, this requires a level of investment and expertise which most projects are unwilling or unable to achieve.

Support services, including transportation assistance and child care, are also very limited. The dislocated worker program only spends a third of the 15 percent of expenditures allowable for support costs, and more than two-fifths of the projects do not provide any support services. Less than a quarter of participants receive services, at an average cost of $196 or between $10-20 per week. Only 2 of 15 projects examined paid stipends, amounting to $50-60 per week.[28]

To sustain dislocated workers while in training, the law prohibits states from denying unemployment insurance benefits to eligible individuals who are enrolled in Title III. However, some states have discouraged assistance to program participants by requiring them to document JTPA enrollment and file individual waivers to qualify for UI benefits. In two of five SDAs surveyed, Title III trainees were either ineligible for UI or else state policy required case by case reviews.[29]

Relocation assistance is offered in isolated cases. Two percent of participants receive such assistance at an average expenditure of about $600. The law limits relocation assistance to individuals who either cannot obtain employment within commuting distance or have a job offer in another locale. For most project participants, relocation is a last resort.[30]

Performance Record

The law requires the department to set standards based on placement and retention in unsubsidized jobs, but lacking an established performance record the Labor Department initially set no national benchmark, and instead required governors to establish their own job placement standards. Governors were also encouraged to implement cost standards.

Based on reports that more than 60 percent of participants entered employment in three-quarters of the states in 1984, the department adopted this rate as a guideline for 1986-7. As in the case of Title IIA, and in spite of the law's requirement that job retention be considered, the job placement guideline does not distinguish between part-time versus full-time or temporary versus permanent jobs. The apparent reason for the department's reluctance to set a definitive standard is the difficulty of collecting representative data on dislocated worker programs. The ad hoc, short-term nature of most dislocated worker projects has hindered the collection of random sample data, without which the standards cannot be fairly adapted to projects facing diverse circumstances and enrollees. Performance standards have apparently had less influence on dislocated worker projects than on Title IIA programs. Half the states do not use performance-based contracts, and only three states rely exclusively on such contracts.[31]

About 69 percent of program terminees found jobs, with hourly wages averaging over $6 at an average cost of $2000 per placement. Job placement performance is similar to the average for adults in Title IIA programs, and the average hourly wage — though below enrollees' previous earnings — is more than a dollar higher. Three of every four who were reemployed found work in four broad occupational categories: [32]

semiskilled equipment or machine operation	34%
skilled crafts or trades	15
clerical or office work	13
service positions	12

Projects operated by unions and/or employers report the highest wage rates, but the reported placement rates of different program operators varied little.[33]

Operator	Hourly wage
Unions and/or employers	$7.62
Service delivery areas	6.70
Educational institutions	5.88
Other public institutions	5.93

The claimed job placement rates for the long-term unemployed, blacks, welfare recipients, dropouts, white males, and unemployment insurance recipients are within a narrow range of 61 to 71 percent. These reported results are baffling, since a much higher differential in placements would normally be expected, but the projects seem to claim success for all comers. Women earn the lowest hourly wages ($5.25), while individuals with more than a high school education earn the most ($7.07).

Performance outcomes differ for various types of training. OJT enrollees achieved the highest placement rates but earned relatively low hourly wages. Classroom and job search training graduates had similar placement and hourly wage rates.

	OJT	Classroom training	Job search assistance
Placement rate	83%	62%	66%
Hourly wage	$6.12	$6.56	$6.40

The reported performance results are subject to serious flaws. In addition to the defects already noted, job placement data do not distinguish between new jobs and recalls of dislocated workers by their former employer. For example, Michigan "achieved" a remarkable 93 percent placement rate with an hourly wage rate averaging $9.47 simply because General Motors recalled about 2000 auto employees who had enrolled in dislocated worker projects.[34]

Trade Politics and Pending Legislation

Alarmed by rising trade deficits exceeding $100 billion annually for three consecutive years, Congress has pushed the trade issue to the forefront of the national agenda. In 1987, to stem protectionist pressures, President Reagan took the unusual step of proposing to consolidate JTPA's Title III and Trade Adjustment Assistance into a new dislocated worker program financed at $980 million for 1988, more than double the $406 million funding received by these programs the previous year.

In an implicit criticism of state management of Title III, the legislative proposals — including the administration's — envisioned expanding both federal and local involvement in the prospective dislocated worker programs. Most policymakers also acknowledged the need to more rapidly respond to mass layoffs and plant closings by obtaining early notice of layoffs from firms and establishing teams to provide technical assistance for rapid implementation of local projects.

Nearly half of the displaced workers surveyed by the U.S. Bureau of Labor Statistics received no advance notice of their layoff.[35] Administrators require at least several months to prepare an effective dislocated worker program. Congress should require large firms to provide at least three months notice of mass layoffs. The U.S. Office of Technology Assessment found little evidence substantiating business claims that an advance notice requirement would cause serious problems.[36] Even a Reagan administration task force concluded that "advance notification is an essential component of a successful adjustment program."[37]

The Canadian Industrial Adjustment Service is a model program which relies on itinerant teams of experts to help rapidly organize local dislocated worker projects. Ensuring the involvement and cooperation of both management and labor as well as community agencies is a key element in the program, a strategy of proven worth in U.S. projects as well.[38] The U.S. Department of Labor is now undertaking a pilot project testing the Canadian approach, and Title III reform proposals incorporate this model.

Additional funding should improve the cost-effectiveness of Title III, as most projects have less than 100 enrollees at a time, far too few to operate efficient programs. The added funds could also enhance the impact of the program by making it possible for administrators to target assistance to the most disadvantaged displaced workers; substantially increase training, basic education, and support services; and improve data collection.

6

The Job Corps
Investing Pays Off

A product of the Great Society's antipoverty efforts, the Job Corps is the nation's oldest continuous federal youth training program. Its high costs have prompted continuing scrutiny, but by the early 1980s the program's accomplishments were acknowledged across the political spectrum. The Job Corps' statutory goal is "to assist young individuals who need and can benefit from an unusually intensive program, operated in a group setting, to become more responsible, employable, and productive citizens."

The program operates residential centers in the belief that removing poor youth from their debilitating environment is a necessary precondition to improving employability. The model reflects the view that poor individuals are trapped in an intergenerational "culture of poverty" which can be best combated through intensive services to youth. Having profited from experience, the Job Corps' effectiveness has improved since the program was established in 1964, but its basic structure has changed little under JTPA. It remains a federally-administered program. Throughout its history, the corps has provided extremely disadvantaged youths with basic education and vocational training, followed by job placement assistance after leaving a center.

Several states operate year-round youth corps programs which are similar to the Job Corps, spending approximately $100 million annually to assist some 15,000 enrollees. The $44 million California Conservation Corps, which operates both residential and nonresidential camps, is the largest state effort. State and local youth corps pursue a broad variety of educational and vocational goals. Although many state and local programs do not restrict eligibility to poor youth, enrollees are primarily disadvantaged.[1]

Administration and Financing

As of mid-1987, the Job Corps funded 105 centers. Businesses and nonprofit organizations administered 75 centers under contract, while the federal Departments of Agriculture and the Interior operated 30 civilian conservation centers (CCCs), modeled upon the New Deal's Civilian Conservation Corps. CCCs emphasize construction and natural resource projects and are located on public lands, primarily in national parks and forests. Contract centers operate in both urban and rural locales.

Nearly three-quarters of Job Corps centers and training slots are located in the South and West (table 6.1).[2] Because many eligible youth do not live in close proximity to Job Corps centers, only a little over half of enrollees are assigned to centers in their home states.[3] The law limits nonresidential trainees to no more than a tenth of participants, and approximately this proportion of nonresidents are enrolled each year. Currently no center is strictly nonresidential.

Table 6.1
Relatively few Job Corps centers are located in
the Northeast and Midwest (1987).

	Number		Distribution		
	Contract centers	Civilian conservation centers	All centers	Training slots	Low income 16-21-year-olds (1980)
South	35	12	45%	49%	37%
West	16	11	26	24	21
Midwest	11	5	15	14	23
Northeast	13	2	14	13	20

Sources: U.S. Department of Labor and Abt Associates, Inc.

The training capacity of the centers varies widely, from 100 to 2600 slots. Centers which can train over 500 corpsmembers at a time constitute a fifth of all centers but serve almost half of total enrollees (figure 6.1). All of the 30 civilian conservation centers and a quarter of the contract centers have a capacity of less than 250 slots, reducing their ability to operate administratively efficient training programs. The six largest private contractors operate 48 centers and train three-fifths of enrollees.

Distribution

	Centers	Training slots	Average center capacity
Civilian conservation centers	29%	16%	213
Six largest private operators	46	58	490
Other private operators	26	27	407

The major source of program instability has been widely fluctuating funding support and attempts by Presidents Nixon and Reagan to abolish the corps, resulting in capacity enrollment ranging from 25,000 to 40,000. In inflation-adjusted 1986 dollars, Job Corps funding reached over $1 billion in 1966, but dropped to $300 million in the mid-1970s (figure 6.2). Financing rose initially following President Carter's inauguration but declined again, subsequently increasing when the administration made reducing youth unemployment a major domestic priority. Since 1981, constant

Figure 6.1
Twenty-one centers train nearly half of all corpsmembers.

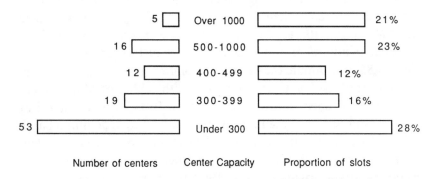

Source: U.S. Department of Labor, Employment and Training Administration

dollar funding for the Job Corps has ranged from $600 to $680 million. Center enrollment capacity has closely followed the available funding.

Figure 6.2
Job Corps appropriations have fluctuated
since the program began.

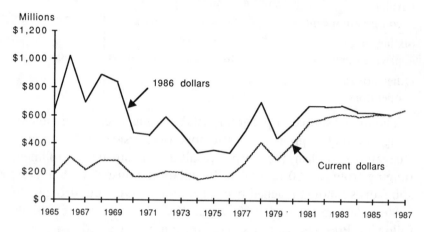

Source: U.S. Department of Labor, Employment and Training Administration

On its 20th anniversary in 1984, President Reagan gave the program a glowing endorsement, stating, "Your vital program has provided hundreds of thousands of deprived youths with basic educational and vocational training to prepare them for their future in the workplace. This is in keeping with the American spirit of helping others reach their full potential, a spirit that has sustained our Nation from its very founding."[4] However, several months later the Reagan administration executed an about-face and proposed in early 1985 to eliminate the program. Congress remained steadfast in its support of the Job Corps and rejected the Office of Management and Budget's repeated attempts to reduce Job Corps funding. For 1987, Congress raised the funding by 7 percent to $656 million and, acknowledging defeat, the administration proposed a nearly identical $652 million budget for the following year. The House of Representatives voted to boost 1988 Job Corps funding to $783 million.

The administration's efforts to eliminate or scale back the Job Corps, while unsuccessful, nevertheless diminished the program's cost-effectiveness. The program's utilization rate, a measurement of average center enrollment compared to capacity, declined from over 99 percent in 1983 and the first half of 1984 to about 95 percent in 1984-5, increasing costs by about $600 per corpsmember service year. Job Corps director Peter Rell testified before a congressional committee that the efforts to end the program were "the major reason" behind recruitment difficulties, because young people were wary of enrolling in a program which might imminently close.[5]

Labor Department staff reductions further impaired federal administration. From 1980 to 1987 federal Job Corps personnel diminished by over a third, from 294 to 190. Three business Job Corps operators protested the effects of the personnel cuts on the program's effectiveness, and one, RCA, criticized the "drastic decrease in the level and quality of technical assistance." The business representatives also noted that the Labor Department's annual program reviews, designed to improve center operations, have become more cursory.[6] These criticisms were substantiated in a leaked internal Labor Department memorandum on the Job Corps which concluded, "It seems clear from all indications that we are not doing a fully adequate job of monitoring." The memo also acknowledged that the Department "practically eliminated" training and technical assistance contracts which had supplemented departmental staff assistance to centers.[7]

Job Corps costs are far higher than those of other JTPA programs, primarily because of the expenses associated with operating residential facilities (figure 6.3 and table 6.2). The cost per training year (the cost of serving a corpsmember for a year) declined steadily between the start of the program and the late 1970s, as two administrations deferred needed capital improvements and permitted health care and allowance expenses to fall behind the cost-of-living. Rectification of these problems and the expansion of the program raised corps costs slightly until the early 1980s.[8] From 1982 to 1985 inflation-adjusted costs per training year declined by 2 percent.

Figure 6.3
The Job Corps' high costs are primarily due to
residential expenses (1985).

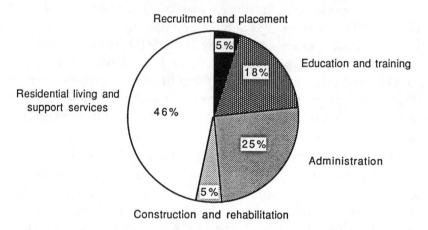

Source: U.S. Department of Labor, Employment and Training Administration

Despite cost reductions over the past two decades, continued high costs — $15,800 per training year in 1985 — have prompted efforts to improve cost efficiency and repeated attempts to close or contract-out the civilian conservation centers, which are more costly. Excluding expenses over which centers have little control (e.g., allowances, construction, recruitment and placement), costs per training year in 1984 ranged from $8300 to $20,000 across centers. The differences were primarily attributable to salaries and economies of scale.[9]

Center capacity	Cost per training year
Under 300	$10,751
300-700	10,185
Over 700	9,394

Even after controlling for size, CCC costs per training year were 40 percent more than at contract centers because of higher vocational training and residential living costs. Higher staff costs account for more than half the differential. The costs of union instructors constitute 65 percent of the difference in training

Table 6.2.
Job Corps Costs (1985)

	Cost	Distribution	Cost per training year
	(millions)		
Total*	**$602.1**	**100.0%**	**$15,731**
National administration	$ 3.5	0.6%	$ 92
Recruitment and placement	32.0	5.3	835
Residential living and support	278.9	46.3	7,286
Salaries	79.2	13.2	2,070
Enrollee allowances	72.8	12.1	1,902
Food	33.1	5.5	866
Energy, utilities, and telephones	28.9	4.8	756
Medical and dental	22.0	3.7	575
Leases and maintenance	16.6	2.8	434
Clothing	13.7	2.3	357
Recreation	5.0	0.8	132
Miscellaneous	7.5	1.2	195
Education	29.1	4.8	760
Salaries	25.4	4.2	663
Miscellaneous	3.7	0.6	96
Vocational training	73.8	12.2	1,928
Salaries	53.2	8.8	1,391
Work experience projects	11.4	1.9	298
Miscellaneous	9.1	1.5	238
Equipment (including educational and vocational)	7.2	1.2	189
Center administration	148.4	24.6	3,877
Salaries	81.0	13.4	2,117
Contractor profit	12.3	2.0	321
Miscellaneous	55.1	9.1	1,439
Construction, rehabilitation, and acquisition	29.3	4.9	765

Source: U.S. Department of Labor, Employment and Training Administration

*Due to different reporting sources, these totals differ slightly from data cited earlier.

expenditures, and higher residential costs are explained by civil service salaries and costlier food expenditures (56 and 32 percent of the difference, respectively).

CCC enrollees experienced better labor market success than contract center corpsmembers in 1984:

	Placement rate	Hourly wage rate
Civilian conservation centers	84%	$4.47
Contract centers	71	3.91

However, a comparison of relative training expenses (excluding equipment) in 1982 indicates that the superior performance of CCCs may not be commensurate with the costs.[10] Moreover, CCC enrollees are probably slightly more advantaged.

Job Corps Enrollees

Recruitment and Screening

Unlike other JTPA components, the Job Corps has sought consistently to limit enrollment to poor youths who face impediments to employment. The Job Corps' high costs, the nature of the target population, and the difficulties inherent in a residential program necessitate a careful selection process. The law requires that applicants must be

- 14 to 21 years old (although in practice only 16-21-year-olds are accepted);

- economically disadvantaged and in need of education, training or counseling to secure meaningful employment, meet Armed Forces requirements, or succeed in school or other training programs;

- living in an environment that would "substantially impair prospects for successful participation in other programs providing needed training, education, or assistance;" and

- "be free of medical and behavioral problems so serious that the individual could not adjust to the standards of conduct, discipline, work, and training which the Job Corps involves."

Several of the standards involve highly subjective judgments, requiring staff to single-out individuals who have employment handicaps severe enough to necessitate exceptional assistance but not so debilitating as to preclude success. The screening process is of crucial importance in minimizing the number of enrollees who drop out of the corps. Early leavers receive little benefit and drive up already high residential costs.

Until the early 1980s, most recruitment and screening was performed by public employment offices, but the Labor Department subsequently instituted a more competitive system. All contracts are awarded through competitive bids and provide a fixed price (typically $160 to $240) for each recruit. Currently state and local government agencies, private profit and nonprofit groups, and Job Corps centers augment the recruitment efforts of public employment offices.

Although the corps often pays recruiters a premium for enlisting women, it continues to experience difficulties attracting women to the program. Parental reluctance to allow their teenage daughters to enroll in a residential program, as well as the fact that prospective female corpsmembers are more likely to be single parents, probably contribute to problems in recruiting women. Congress, in 1982, ordered the department to "immediately take steps to achieve" 50 percent female enrollment, but the proportion of women instead fell from 38 to 32 percent during the succeeding four years.

A persistent criticism of recruiters centers on their lack of effort to determine if applicants could be better served by alternative programs. Congress intended the Job Corps to be a last resort for youth whose living environment impairs their employment and education prospects. In 1979, the U.S. General Accounting Office concluded that the program's screening was so lax that "nearly any disadvantaged youth can qualify." GAO noted that an inadequate eligibility determination procedure had characterized the corps since its inception.[11] More recent investigations indicate that the problems GAO enumerated continue.[12] However, while it is clear that Job Corps screening has not satisfied the letter of the law, the characteristics of corpsmembers indicate that recruiters generally enforce the law's intent.

Characteristics

The Job Corps' clientele has remained remarkably similar over the years. The average corpsmember reads at the 6th grade level. Almost three of four have never held a full-time job. Four of five are high school dropouts, and nearly half of their families receive welfare (table 6.3).

Female enrollees generally have completed more schooling than males. One of four female enrollees has completed the 12th grade, compared to about one of fifteen men. One of six female and one of twenty male enrollees are nonresidents. Nonresidential corpsmembers have completed slightly more years of schooling than residential enrollees, but their entry reading levels are nearly identical. Eighteen percent of nonresident enrollees are Hispanic, compared to 8 percent of residents.

The clientele of civilian conservation centers differs markedly from that of contract centers, and is probably less disadvantaged. Half of CCC enrollees are white, compared to only a quarter of contract center enrollees. Only one in ten CCC participants is female. Although CCC corpsmembers are slightly younger and have consequently completed less schooling, their entry reading levels are on average a grade higher than contract center participants.[13]

Given the subjectivity of the Job Corps' eligibility requirements, it is possible only to estimate the number of potentially eligible individuals. About one million of the approximately four million disadvantaged 16-21-year-olds are high school dropouts. An additional but unknown proportion are deficiently educated graduates. Like other job training programs, the 100,000 annual enrollees represent a fraction of those potentially eligible. However, due to the program's residential nature only a minority of the eligible youth wish to enroll.

Table 6.3
Most corpsmembers are minority high school dropouts
with severely deficient reading skills (1985).

Characteristics	Percent
Sex	
Male	68.2%
Female	31.8
Age at entry	
16	19.5
17	20.3
18	20.0
19	17.6
20	12.5
21	8.5
Over 21	1.6
Race	
Black	56.9
White	28.2
Hispanic	8.9
Indian	3.9
Other	2.1
Highest grade completed	
1-7th grade	4.7
8th grade	13.5
9th grade	22.8
10th grade	22.1
11th grade	16.5
12th grade or more	20.4
Entry reading level	
Under grade 3	7.7
Grades 3-4	23.8
Grades 5-6	30.9
Grades 7-8	23.9
Above grade 8	13.7

Source: U.S. Department of Labor, Employment and Training Administration

Upon arriving at a center, the new corpsmember receives a week-long orientation explaining the educational and vocational programs, residential rules, health services and recreational activities. Most of the centers assign a veteran corpsmember to each new enrollee to facilitate his or her transition to center life. The average enrollee remains at a center for seven months, but a third leave within three months (figure 6.4).

Figure 6.4
A major problem of the Job Corps is that half the enrollees remain in the centers for less than six months (1985).

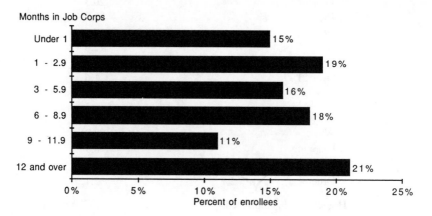

Source: U.S. Departmentof Labor, Employment and Training Administration

Education

Centers organize the educational and vocational programs by dividing the day in half for each track, alternating weeks, or using both methods depending upon the occupational training course.[14] In 22 centers examined, 10 used a split-day schedule, 6 alternated weeks, and 6 used a combination schedule. The split-day schedule is more advantageous to enrollees, who have problems under the alternating week schedule in sustaining their attention for a full day of educational instruction and retaining course material during the off week. Centers which alternate weeks of educational and vocational instruction do so primarily to accommodate commuting vocational instructors.

Basic Education

Over four-fifths of corpsmembers have completed the 9th grade, but only 14 percent read at that level. However, entry-level abilities range from the functionally illiterate to those who can read fairly well. Therefore, instructors first administer standardized tests to determine at what level corpsmembers should begin their reading and math program. In addition to the placement test, the Labor Department recently required centers to administer adult basic education tests to all new enrollees to uniformly gauge educational gains.

To accommodate divergent reading abilities, Job Corps reading instruction is individualized. Enrollees move through a series of short, competency-based lessons, progressing to the next lesson only after passing a test to ensure proficiency. Individuals proceed at their own pace and are assisted by instructors when they need help. Basic course materials are standardized, but the Labor Department encourages centers to test innovative and experimental approaches, and the Job Corps has pioneered in developing instructional materials for youth and adults who failed in or were failed by the schools.

Lack of confidence and motivation typically compound corpsmembers' reading difficulties. Although the program deemphasizes competition between enrollees, staff report that poor readers often feel stigmatized by other corpsmembers. Centers are not equipped to deal with learning disabilities, and individuals with severe disabilities are usually terminated from the program. Many enrollees are more interested in occupational training than education, and participants' interest and progress often lag when they do not see the relevance of schooling to their careers. Consequently, educational and vocational instructors often work together to resolve occupational training problems attributable to poor reading skills.

The Job Corps' reading program is remarkably successful in comparison to traditional schooling techniques, although the centers have been slow to utilize computer-assisted instruction, probably because of financial impediments. Recent achievement tests indicate that corpsmembers on average gain about two months of reading achievement for every month of instruction. Thus enrollees not only perform dramatically better than they had in school, but outpace average student performance. The average corpsmember, enrolled in the program for seven to eight months, probably progresses from a 6th grade reading ability to a 7th or 8th grade level. Although the Labor Department has required centers to maintain records of participants' reading gains, a 1985 study found that reporting was so inadequate that "no reliable data" existed to assess reading improvement.[15] However, since that time the department has revised its instructions, requiring centers to use a uniform standardized test to assess corpsmember educational progress.

Some centers offer courses in English as a second language, primarily for the Hispanic, Vietnamese, Cambodian and Laotian corpsmembers who account for about a tenth of enrollees. These individuals usually remain in ESL programs until their English is adequate for educational and vocational training, which typically takes six months to a year. The Labor Department does not report the average length of stay for ESL enrollees, but it is probable that many do not remain long enough to complete an occupational training course.

Most new enrollees' math skills do not extend much beyond basic addition and subtraction. Instructors estimate that 40-60 percent of new corpsmembers have difficulty with fractions, measurements, percentages and decimals. The math program offers individualized and self-paced instruction designed to make corpsmembers proficient in consumer math. Unlike the program's other education courses, the math curriculum is based primarily on commercially published texts rather than on Job Corps materials, although some supplementary exercises have been developed specifically for the program.

Math instructors generally encounter few problems teaching from the standardized curriculum, although, as in the reading program, teachers commonly use supplementary materials. Math education is linked to some degree with vocational training, particularly in labs where students practice measurement exercises. Teachers also work informally with vocational instructors when corpsmembers face training difficulties attributable to deficient math skills.

High School Equivalency and Beyond

Enrollees who attain 8th or 9th grade reading proficiency enter the high school equivalency degree program. The Job Corps has designed a special curriculum for the program, although many instructors supplement this material and a fifth of the instructors questioned were so dissatisfied with the curriculum that they did not use it at all.

Evaluations of the Job Corps demonstrate that attainment of an equivalency degree has a significant impact on later employment success and educational achievement.[16] However, only about a seventh of the enrollees take the General Education Development (GED) test. Ninety percent of those who take the test pass it.

Several factors partially explain the limited number of corpsmembers who take the test. A fifth of new enrollees in 1985 had completed the 12th grade. Most of these individuals probably already possessed a diploma or equivalency degree, and in fact only 4 percent took the GED while in the corps. A third of enrollees leave the program within three months, and it takes about that much time to complete GED instruction. However, even of those who had not completed the 12th grade and stayed in the Job Corps longer than six months, less than a third take the GED test. Not even half of those staying over a year take the test. One study examined the correlation between entry reading level and GED attainment for corpsmembers who had completed grades 9 through 11 and remained in the program for over six months. The distribution follows:

Entry reading level	Obtained GED
Less than 7th grade	16%
7th to 8th grade	46
9th grade or higher	65

Although the Job Corps' GED program has improved considerably in recent years — the proportion of enrollees obtaining equivalency degrees has doubled since the late 1970s — more emphasis on securing equivalency degrees for corpsmembers is necessary.[17] The limited number of long-term participants who receive certificates suggests that the record can be further improved. In late 1986, the

Job Corps instituted a GED performance standard to promote the high school equivalency program.

Corpsmembers who complete their vocational program and attain a high school diploma or equivalency degree may receive postsecondary education or training through the corps' advanced career training program. Begun in 1979 to encourage lengthier program stays and provide a career ladder for outstanding achievers, the Labor Department canceled the program in 1981 but revived it three years later. Currently, 30 centers contract with a variety of private vocational schools and community colleges to train about 2 percent of corpsmembers at an annual cost of $1.5 million.

Health and Consumer Instruction

In addition to math and reading courses, Job Corps centers provide health and "World of Work" education. The latter program offers training in job search skills and consumer education, typically beginning at the same time as the math and reading classes and lasting 30 to 40 hours over a two- to eight-week period. Because the World of Work program is typically completed within a few months of enrollment, most centers offer a 5-15 hour refresher course for corpsmembers preparing to leave the center.

Although the curriculum is standardized, the health education program offers group rather than individualized instruction designed to help enrollees make informed decisions about their health needs. The program usually begins within a month and a half after corpsmembers arrive at the center, and provides 27 lessons for an average of 32 hours instruction.

Instructors

Job Corps teachers' salaries and benefits are inferior to working conditions in local schools. Entry-level teacher salaries at the centers are 15-20 percent below starting wages at area schools, although corps instructors face a longer workday and a 12-month working year. However, centers report few difficulties in recruiting competent instructors because many teachers are attracted by a program that offers a strict disciplinary system and the challenge of teaching students who failed in or were failed by the established educational system. An oversupply of qualified teachers in recent years has also benefited the program.

As government civil service employees, teachers at civilian conservation centers are better paid than contract center instructors, but civil service procedures delay processing of hiring new teachers by as much as two to six months. The lowest paid CCC instructor makes about as much as the highest paid teachers at contract centers. The latter usually leave after three to five years for a better paying job, while many CCC instructors have over 10 years tenure.

Vocational Training

Job Corps enrollees' work histories are commensurate with their limited educational achievements. Seventy percent have never held a full-time job, and another 12 percent have previously worked full time but not within six months of enrollment. Half of those who had held full-time jobs earned the minimum wage or less.

Shortly after enrolling, each corpsmember participates in a three- to five-day vocational orientation program and learns about the training opportunities at the center. However, fewer than half of the centers provide new enrollees with some hands-on exposure to various trades, and instructors believe that a more intensive orientation is necessary to allow enrollees to make informed vocational choices. Vocational assignment is generally determined by corpsmember preference, and four of five corpsmembers are assigned to their first vocational choice.[18]

The Job Corps offers training in about 120 occupations, although each center typically offers only 8-10. Four of five corpsmembers are trained for one of eleven occupations:

clerk typist or secretary	9.3%
cook or baker	9.1
welder	8.8
nurse's or medical assistant	8.8
auto repair	8.7
carpenter	8.2

general or sales clerk	8.0
custodial or maintenance	6.7
mason	6.5
painter	3.4
electrician	3.0

The remainder of the training opportunities represent a wide variety of occupations. About half of these require relatively few skills, such as keypunch operator, warehouseman and receptionist, while the others are more skilled jobs, such as accountant or appliance repair person.

Occupational enrollment reflects traditional gender patterns. Most women are trained to be clerk typists, nurse's aides, cooks, or clerks. Greater variety is generally available to men, in addition to the listed occupations. The Labor Department's comprehensive review of the program's offerings in 1983 concluded that Job Corps trades correlated well with occupational demand projections. The review panel recommended 12 new offerings, including computer and health-related trades, and several of these occupations were added by 1987. High initial investment costs inhibit new vocational offerings.

Center operators provide most of the training. In addition, the Washington Job Corps office selects national contractors, usually labor unions, to provide some training. Each service provider offers training for distinctly different occupations. For example, almost 80 percent of national contractor training is for construction trades, provided primarily by carpenters', masons' and painters' unions. In 1982 contract center instructors provided training for 75 percent of the 32,000 enrollees who spent over three months in the program, national contractors taught 16 percent, and civilian conservation center instructors trained the remaining 9 percent of enrollees. CCCs rely heavily on national contractors to provide training, while the contract centers commonly use in-house staff. Both kinds of centers also use local subcontractors for a small proportion of training.[19]

Like Job Corps education courses, much of the vocational training program is individualized and self-paced, consisting of a series of competency-based lessons. The adequacy of facilities and equipment varies from center to center, with the larger centers being generally better equipped. Some of the smaller centers have outdated or insufficient equipment, most commonly for construction, clerical, automotive and welding courses. In 1980, the Job Corps began a major overhaul of its vocational program to establish standardized courses which stress the basic skills necessary to perform in each occupation. Industry and training experts as well as Job Corps personnel designed the courses, which were then tested at selected centers. Implementation of the new system, which will encompass all major occupational offerings, is scheduled to be completed in 1988.

Although hands-on experience is considered an important element of the Job Corps' vocational program, opportunities for learning while doing are not uniformly available across occupations. Corpsmembers training in the construction, automotive, and industrial production trades tend to receive the most hands-on experience in actual or simulated settings, while health, clerical and sales training is more classroom oriented.

The centers generally have little difficulty recruiting and retaining vocational instructors, but face somewhat greater problems than the education program experiences. Salaries of CCC and national contractor instructors are at least comparable with similar private sector jobs, which results in extremely low turnover. Although the wages offered by contract centers are not as generous, they too experience minimal recruitment and turnover problems because the steady work hours offered by the program attracts instructors.[20]

The Residential Living Program

The most unique feature about the Job Corps is its residential nature.[21] The program's designers believed that providing a structured and supportive living environment was essential to break the "cycle of poverty" trapping many impoverished youngsters, but this theory is by no means universally accepted. Disentangling the elements which account for the Job Corps' success is no easy task. The most recent net impact study of the program included only residential enrollees because, when the study began in 1977, very few enrollees lived outside the centers. Moreover, differences between the two types of enrollees preclude simple comparisons of postprogram outcomes.

A demonstration project underway in mid-1987, called Jobstart, is designed to replicate the Job Corps approach in a nonresidential setting. Seventeen- to 21-year-old dropouts from impoverished homes with limited reading skills were randomly assigned to either Jobstart training or a control group in late 1985 and 1986. Jobstart involves 15 sites, 11 administered by local JTPA Title II agencies and 4 by Job Corps centers. All sites are to provide at least 5.5 months of instruction, significantly less than the Job Corps' average in recent years of seven to eight months, which may complicate assessments of the project.[22]

Operating a residential program poses a severe challenge for both Job Corps staff and participants. Corpsmembers must adjust to living in a new environment away from home while pursuing a disciplined education and training program, an especially difficult challenge for troubled youngsters lacking self-confidence. Many corpsmembers fail again, and either drop out or are dismissed from the program.

Corpsmembers receive living allowances of $40 to $100 monthly based on duration of enrollment as well as performance.

Monthly allowance	Duration	Proportion of enrollees (November 1986)
$ 40	Entry to 2 months	32%
$ 60	2-6 months	32
$ 80	After 6 months	14
$ 90	Merit allowance	7
$100	Merit allowance	14

Success or failure in the program often hinges upon whether new enrollees can adjust to group living. Housing accommodations in various centers range from a barracks to college-type dorm rooms. Anywhere from 2 to 42 enrollees sleep in a single room, although 8 or less is typical. Staff and corpsmembers share housekeeping chores. A staff of resident advisers (RAs) living in the dorms is responsible for acclimating enrollees to center life and minimizing behavioral problems, including drinking and fighting. The RAs play a crucial role in maintaining discipline. Center officials report that a drop in the number of RAs below a critical threshold is associated with unacceptable levels of misbehavior.

Extensive counseling also helps corpsmembers adjust to center life. Homesickness is a universal problem, and enrollees also receive individual and group counseling for a wide variety of personal, educational and vocational difficulties. Most contract centers schedule regular group counseling sessions fairly often, usually every week, which are supplemented with monthly individual counseling. In contrast, at CCCs most counseling is provided informally by RAs. Formal counseling is generally used only when a corpsmember requests it or a teacher or RA makes a referral.

Job Corps staff consider the recreational program a vital tool in channeling the energy of enrollees into acceptable activities. Corpsmembers themselves plan and operate most recreational activities — which include team sports, dances, parties, and center stores or snack bars — to ensure that they are appealing.

All centers have elected corpsmember governments, varying from moribund bodies to those extensively involved in almost all facets of center activities. Not surprisingly, corpsmember governments are most interested in recreational programs and food service. The Labor Department also requires each center to encourage leadership potential. More gifted corpsmembers are enrolled in a leadership training course lasting from 6 to 40 hours, and then assigned work as aides in classrooms, recreational facilities, offices and shops. In return for extra responsibilities and work, the individual receives special privileges such as living in an honor dorm, use of recreational facilities outside normal hours, and passes to leave the center.

Corpsmembers receive comprehensive health care to ensure that medical problems do not inhibit their progress in the program. Each center has a full-time nurse or medical technician, and those centers without a staff doctor establish consulting arrangements with outside physicians. In addition to routine medical services, almost all centers operate alcohol and drug abuse and pregnancy programs. Job Corps staff at various centers estimate that 1-10 percent of female participants arrive pregnant at centers, and a small proportion become pregnant while enrolled. Pregnant corpsmembers generally remain in the program until the seventh month of pregnancy.

Life at the centers is fairly regimented. Attendance is carefully monitored, and enrollees must obtain passes to leave the center for any reason. Staff conduct periodic inspections of both living and storage areas, and about half the centers routinely search all packages coming in or out of the facilities to keep out alcohol and drugs. If a crime is committed, most security officers try to handle the matter internally unless it involves a serious offense. Centers which rely on informal procedures have some difficulty levying consistent sanctions for like offenses.

Almost all centers use trained security personnel. Demands on these employees vary greatly between centers, with some expected to provide counseling while others merely follow formal security procedures. Because salaries are not competitive with local security agencies, the Job Corps experiences difficulty in recruiting and retaining qualified security personnel.

Running the residential program is a demanding job requiring a diversity of skills. The staff is primarily composed of residential advisors and counselors, although the duties associated with each of these positions vary greatly across centers. There is approximately one residential staff member for every eleven enrollees, a ratio which varies little among centers.

RAs at some centers (especially CCCs) do a great deal of counseling, while others primarily perform custodial work. In contrast to most positions at Job Corps centers, RAs and related jobs such as dorm attendants are subject to fairly high turnover. Salaries are generally low, and many RAs are college students or else take the position as a second job. Almost half the centers examined in 1984 experienced an average annual RA turnover rate of 35 percent.

Job Corps counselors are better paid but face diverse duties. Counselors are supposed to advise corpsmembers on their educational and vocational goals as well as personal problems. In addition to their therapeutic duties, counselors also typically manage the performance evaluation panels which monitor corpsmember progress. Professional qualifications are minimal considering the demands placed on counselors. Only 1 of 23 centers examined in 1984 required a master's degree — a bachelor's degree in psychology or sociology was usually acceptable. To assist counselors, the national office requires each center to hire a mental health consultant to be available for a few hours a week to advise or train counselors and to accept referrals of particularly difficult cases.

The Dropout Problem

Ensuring that as many new entrants as possible complete the program is critical to the success of the Job Corps. Over the years, the Job Corps has greatly diminished the proportion of early leavers, but the problem remains serious. The Job Corps is a voluntary program, and enrollees are free to leave when they wish. The average stay in the centers is 7.2 months, but a third of participants leave within 3 months, half of these within the first month. By minimizing early departures and providing more intensive training, the Job Corps has nearly doubled average training duration since the program began (figure 6.5). Program completers now stay, on average, over a year in the Job Corps.

Figure 6.5
The average stay in the Job Corps has increased significantly.

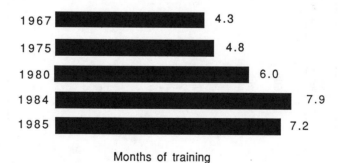

Months of training

Source: U.S. Department of Labor, Employment and Training Administration

Despite the improvements, only a third of enrollees completed the program in 1985 (table 6.4). Women are more likely to leave for

Table 6.4
Most corpsmembers do not complete their training program (1985).*

	Male residents	Male nonresidents	Female residents	Female nonresidents	Total	Average stay (months)
Terminations	37,600	3,300	16,100	3,500	60,500	7.2
Average stay (months)	6.8	10.5	7.3	8.2	7.2	-
Reasons						
Completed program	28.7%	53.7%	34.6%	40.2%	32.3%	13.5
Quit	49.1	37.5	48.3	52.1	48.5	3.9
Resigned	30.1	20.2	28.8	25.2	29.0	4.6
AWOL	19.0	17.3	19.5	26.9	19.5	2.9
Left for disciplinary reasons	16.2	4.5	8.3	1.4	12.6	5.3
Medical	1.9	.8	4.5	1.9	2.5	4.1
Withdrawal of parental consent	2.2	.7	2.6	.3	2.1	2.1
Administrative	1.5	2.1	1.2	2.1	1.5	3.9

Source: U.S. Department of Labor, Employment and Training Administration

*Details do not total 100 percent because reasons for 0.5 percent of terminations are unrecorded.

medical reasons (primarily due to pregnancy) and less likely to depart for disciplinary infractions than men. Nonresidents are much more likely to complete the program than residents, partly because they do not face the pressures and regimentation of center life. In 1985, 35 percent of residents compared with 25 percent of nonresidents remained less than three months in the Job Corps. Residents are more likely to depart for disciplinary reasons because most serious incidents occur after hours when nonresidents have left for the day.

Corpsmembers who leave without notice usually stay in the program for less than three months and constitute the bulk of the early leaver problem. Corpsmembers have indicated the following principal reasons for early departures:[23]

- homesickness;
- an inability to adjust to the Job Corps' structure and rules;
- insufficient pay;
- poor screening by recruiters; and
- enrollees' inability to make decisions about their interests and goals.

Interviews with center staff confirm many of these impressions. Staff view homesickness as the most important reason for dropping out within the first month, and an inability to adjust to center life as the principal explanation for those leaving in the second or third month. Lack of privacy, racial and ethnic animosities, regimentation, and bullying or assaults are the most common adjustment problems.

Younger corpsmembers are more prone to drop out early, and the likelihood decreases with age. During 1984, 34 percent of 16-year-olds compared with 23.5 percent of 21-year-olds left the program within three months. Similarly, only two-fifths of the youngest corpsmembers stay over six months, compared to three-fifths of the 21-year-olds. Job Corps administrators have long known that younger enrollees are prone to drop out, and over the years the average age of the corpsmembers has increased: a little over a decade ago nearly two-thirds of enrollees were under 18, compared with 40 percent currently. To improve the cost efficiency of the Job Corps, a persuasive case can be made for excluding 16-year-olds from the program.

Whites — who are a minority in the centers — are much more likely than ethnic or racial minorities to leave the Job Corps within three months:

Whites	38%
American Indians	32
Hispanics	31
Blacks	25
Asians	8

The likelihood of whites dropping out is increased for those assigned to predominantly black centers. Over a quarter of the whites assigned to centers with over 70 percent black enrollment leave within the first month, compared to 16 percent of the whites assigned to other centers. Interestingly, the white dropout rate does not differ for the two types of centers in the second and third month of enrollment, which may indicate that white dropouts are uncomfortable in a black environment rather than that racial tensions constitute a persistent problem.

Enrollees at civilian conservation centers are more likely to stay in the program over three months than those at contract centers. The size and location of a center, corpsmember gender, and whether enrollees are assigned to their preferred occupational training program apparently have little impact on the dropout problem.[24]

The Labor Department and center operators have reduced the numbers of early leavers through various techniques. Recruiters are expected to carefully screen potential enrollees for serious medical and behavioral problems, and the Labor Department audits recruiters who refer too many unsuitable applicants. The referral of clearly ineligible applicants to centers is apparently not a serious problem. The 2.5 percent of corpsmembers terminated for medical reasons had been in the program for an average of four months, making it unlikely that many of these medical problems predated admittance to the Job Corps. Similarly, since the 1.5 percent of enrollees terminated for administrative reasons (including ineligibility as well as a failure to make sufficient progress) had also typically been in the program for four months, it is doubtful that many were admitted due to poor screening. Moreover, some screening errors are attributable to false information provided by applicants who conceal mental health problems or criminal records from recruiters. Legal restrictions often prevent recruiters from independently verifying this kind of information.

While recruiters apparently enlist few ineligible applicants, they often fail to fully explain the program to applicants, which significantly contributes to the dropout problem, according to both center staff and corpsmembers. A recent evaluation found significant variations between recruitment agencies in the accuracy and completeness of information they possessed concerning individual centers. The recruiters were generally knowledgeable about center training programs, but often lacked information about center living conditions, recreational programs, health facilities, and the surrounding community. Many recruiters had not visited the centers for which they solicited applicants, and were therefore dependent upon the centers' promotional literature, hardly an unbiased source. Some recruiters did not even possess copies of the corpsmember handbooks produced by each center.

Job Corps centers use various approaches to minimize the number of dropouts. Center staff commonly phone prospective enrollees to ensure that they have been informed about center living conditions, know what training opportunities are available, and are genuinely committed to the program. Many centers have a big brother or sister program to help orient new enrollees, and several make dormitory assignments with an eye toward ensuring racial balance and minimizing bullying. Counseling staff try to spot problems which might lead to early departures, and minimize homesickness by permitting calls and visits home.[25]

Postprogram Experiences

Placement assistance

Upon leaving a center, corpsmembers are provided job search assistance and a readjustment allowance. Until 1985, public employment offices provided most of the job search assistance in about four-fifths of the states, but by competitively bidding placement contracts the national office has expanded the role of alternative

organizations. Job Corps centers, a state human resource department, private corporations, Wider Opportunities for Women (a
community-based organization), and the United Auto Workers
now augment the employment service network. All agencies are
now paid a fixed fee for every job placement, replacing the previous
practice of reimbursing for all expenditures whether or not a
placement resulted.

Upon a corpsmember's departure, the Job Corps center notifies
the responsible placement agency that the former enrollee is due to
arrive in the area. Contact is facilitated because corpsmembers can
only pick up their readjustment allowance at the agency office, and
over 90 percent of terminees are located. Corpsmembers who stayed
in the program at least six months receive $75 for each of the first
six months, and $100 for each month over six. Terminees who
remained in the corps more than nine months are paid $100 for each
month they were enrolled.

Since they are judged partially by their alumni placement record,
some centers offer placement assistance, complementing the work
of the placement agencies over which they have little control. The
remote locations of civilian conservation centers generally render
placement efforts impractical, but some contract centers use their
work experience program to generate jobs for graduates. National
contractors are especially successful at using their local contacts to
place corpsmembers.

Longer Training Pays Off

Placement agencies report that program completers are relatively
easy to place, while early leavers require considerable assistance.
The Job Corps performance standards reflect this fact. Two of the
standards assess center success in retaining participants. A third
standard gauges the success of long-term enrollees (over six months'
time) in finding work or continuing their education. The Labor
Department has established a range of acceptable performance
rather than a target figure (table 6.5).

Although the national average performance was within the
acceptable range for the three targets, a third of the centers had
overall unacceptable ratings for the year ending in June 1986.
Despite the Labor Department's tough talk on sanctions, no more

than four contracts were terminated due to poor performance. Thus the standards have been used more as guidelines and have probably had limited influence on center operations.

Table 6.5
One of three centers failed to meet the performance standards.

	90+ day retention rate	180+ day retention rate*	180+ day positive termination rate	Total centers	Unacceptable rating
Performance standards					
1985	65-75%	75-83%	80-90%		
1986	64-75	73-80	80-92		
1985 outcomes	66	76	86	105	35
Range	46-94	62-90	63-97	-	-
Program operator					
Agriculture Department	70	77	89	18	3
Interior Department	65	75	90	12	3
Management & Training Corp.	65	77	88	13	2
Singer	71	77	85	11	2
RCA	64	73	87	10	8
Teledyne	67	75	84	7	3
Res-Care, Inc.	63	75	84	5	3
Minact	63	73	80	4	3

Source: U.S. Department of Labor, Employment and Training Administration
*Proportion of 90+day enrollees who remain over 180 days.

The department issued a fourth performance standard in late 1986 designed to encourage attainment of high school equivalency diplomas. Unlike the other benchmarks, the GED standard is applied individually to each center and is based on a regression model which considers the age and reading level of participants, as well as other enrollee and center characteristics. The target gauges equivalency attainment among enrollees who enter the program with at least a fourth grade reading level and are old enough to take the GED test. A model standard of 30 percent GED attainment was chosen based on 1984 performance, and each center must meet the model-adjusted target plus or minus 9 percentage points, but the adjustments cannot lower the standard below a 10 percent GED attainment rate. Using 1986 enrollee and center characteristics, the model produced performance targets ranging from 10 to 38 percent across centers.

A fifth performance standard assessing educational gains was to be issued during 1987. Centers are now required to administer a standardized test to corpsmembers on three "national test days" every year. The department will use the test results to establish minimal educational improvement goals for each center.

The Job Corps' national office has used performance standards in a more creditable manner than other JTPA programs. Performance standards have been applied to accomplishments over which centers have more direct control, such as length of training and educational progress. The corps' performance standard system is also based on more reliable data than that collected in other JTPA programs because centers record, for example, the entry reading levels of enrollees. The fact that a third of the centers failed the 1985 benchmarks indicates a need for either greater enforcement or a recalibration of the standards. Even the performance of the major contractor with the worst record (RCA) was not much different from that of the average center. Other JTPA performance systems could benefit by adopting some of the Job Corps' practices.

The Job Corps' definition of a successful placement is similar to the Title IIA program's positive termination outcome, but without the deficiencies that mar that standard. Corpsmembers who acquire a part-time or full-time job or an on-the-job training position of at least 20 hours a week; enroll full time in a school, training or apprenticeship program; or join the military or national guard within six months of termination are considered successfully placed. Other JTPA programs generally count placements within a three month postprogram period.

The Job Corps' placement reporting practices have raised troubling questions. Until the early 1980s, the program only reported outcomes for corpsmembers it was able to locate. Currently, the corps assumes that unlocated corpsmembers have the same rate of placement success as the recorded group of individuals who receive no assistance from placement agencies. However, this assumption is questionable because performance standards discourage placement agencies from submitting records for individuals not placed. A more serious problem is the failure of the national office to verify reported placements. The Labor Department's inspector general found that about one of four reported placements were spurious in 1982.[26] No similar audits of reported performance have been performed during the past five years.

For the year ending in June 1986, using the corps' estimation procedure, 74 percent of terminees were successfully placed. If only those individuals who were located are counted, the positive termination rate rises to 81 percent, while discarding the estimation technique but including unlocated individuals lowers the rate to 66 percent. Four-fifths of those placed obtained jobs or joined the military, and the remainder entered school. Male enrollees and program completers fare best in the labor market (table 6.6). Former female corpsmembers are more likely to drop out of the labor force to assume family responsibilities, which reduces their positive termination rate. Reported Job Corps outcomes are very similar to the outcomes for the relatively more advantaged youth in the Title IIA program.

Table 6.6
Program completers achieve the best postprogram results (1985).

	Positive termination rate*	Hourly wage
Total	74%	$4.17
Male	77	4.28
Female	68	3.90
Termination Reason		
Completed program	83	4.55
Disciplinary reasons	72	3.89
Resigned	73	3.90
AWOL	69	3.85
Medical	49	3.66
Administrative	64	3.70
Removal of parental consent	71	3.80
Length of Stay		
0-89 days	67	3.80
90-179 days	71	3.92
180+ days	80	4.34

Source: U.S. Department of Labor, Employment and Training Administration

*Data reflect authors' adjustment of Labor Department statistics to account for unlocated terminees.

Enrollees who train to become carpenters, masons, and painters are generally most successful at finding relatively high paying jobs within six months after leaving the corps (table 6.7). The relatively superior outcomes for trainees in these construction trades is probably attributable to two factors. First, a sizable proportion of construction training is offered by national union contractors who have an established employment network for Job Corps graduates. Second, union construction programs tend to select older and relatively more qualified corpsmembers.[27]

The likelihood of completing training or positively terminating from the program does not vary much by training occupation. Job placement and wage rates exhibit more variation; occupations with large numbers of women fare worst in the labor market. Except for clerk typists and secretaries, trainees who remain for longer periods in the program tend to find better paying jobs. Overall, only a third of employed terminees find work in their field of training.

Longer Term Impact

The Job Corps underwent a careful assessment during the late 1970s and early 1980s. The findings convincingly demonstrate the program's worth in improving enrollees' employment prospects, and the evaluations have protected the Job Corps from serious budget cuts despite White House efforts in the 1980s to discredit the program's established record.

A comprehensive study examined the experiences of a random sample of 1977 corpsmembers over a four-year period and a comparison group of youth with similar characteristics. The similarity of the two groups was confirmed by the fact that the experiences of the early Job Corps leavers paralleled those of the comparison group.

The positive impacts of the program, which persisted throughout the four-year follow-up period, were striking. Former corpsmembers had significantly greater employment and earnings, more education, better health, and less serious criminal records than the comparison group. The corpsmembers were also less likely than the comparison group to receive cash welfare payments, food stamps or unemployment insurance. Former enrollees received on average half the amount of cash benefits obtained by members of the

Table 6.7.

Construction trainees achieve greatest labor market success in the short term (1985).

	Trainees	Duration (months)	Completed training	Positive termination rate	Job placement rate	Hourly wage	Job matches training occupation	Percent males
Total	**50,588**	**7.2**	**35%**	**81%**	**66%**	**$4.17**	**35%**	**68%**
Male dominated occupations								
Cook or baker	4,613	6.1	39	80	65	3.84	51	62
Welder	4,442	7.2	37	83	69	4.23	25	93
Auto repair	4,403	6.2	35	85	71	4.13	28	95
Carpenter	4,156	7.5	36	85	74	4.68	46	93
Custodial or maintenance	3,383	6.5	40	83	69	4.13	39	87
Mason	3,280	7.5	33	83	72	4.53	42	95
Painter	1,727	6.9	36	82	71	4.48	41	87
Electrician	1,527	6.9	41	87	76	4.28	44	92
Female dominated occupations								
Clerk typist or secretary	4,692	7.1	41	79	59	3.97	36	21
Nurse's or medical assistant	4,440	6.2	41	78	61	3.76	42	23
General or sales clerk	4,059	6.6	43	79	62	4.01	36	24

Source: U.S. Department of Labor, Employment and Training Administration

Note: Table excludes unlocated terminees.

comparison group. Despite the program's persistent difficulties in securing high school equivalency degrees for enrollees, former corpsmembers were much more likely to have earned diplomas or equivalency degrees than nonparticipants, and more had enrolled in college.

Counting civilian jobs and military enlistments, former corpsmembers worked an average of one and a half weeks more in the first follow-up year than the comparison group, and three to five weeks more in the second through the fourth years. The civilian employment rate was 6 percent higher for corpsmembers. Annual earnings, in 1977 dollars, were $262 higher than nonenrollees' earnings in the first year and $405 to $652 higher in the next three years, about 15 percent higher than the comparison group. Participants' higher earnings were primarily attributable to increased working time rather than to higher wages. The evidence was mixed as to whether the Job Corps' positive employment impact was fading toward the end of the four-year follow-up.

Imputing dollar values to Job Corps benefits — admittedly an inexact science — analysts concluded that the program yields $1.46 for every $1 invested. From a societal perspective, benefits exceeded costs by over $2300 per corpsmember in 1977 dollars ($4200 in 1986 dollars), and the program's investment in the average enrollee was paid back in just three years. Most of Job Corps' benefits were derived from the increased economic output and decreased criminal behavior of corpsmembers.[28]

Interestingly, the program's benefits were not apparent during the year after corpsmembers left the centers, as the alumni had some difficulty readjusting to the outside world, indicating that short-term results may not be a reliable barometer of long-term employment success. Somewhat surprisingly, the study found that general or sales clerk trainees fared best in the long run. Adjusting for participant characteristics, individuals trained as clerks, welders and electricians had the highest earnings, while former corpsmembers in the other principal vocational programs earned at or below the average for all corps alumni (table 6.8). Former painter trainees, who exhibited nearly the best results in the short term, fared poorly in the long run. On the other hand, the former clerk trainees with the highest long-term earnings performed below average in the immediate postprogram period. The findings, while they do not make intuitive sense and bear further investigation, provide further support for cautiously interpreting performance measures based on short-term results.[29]

The evaluators also examined the impact of the program from the perspective of corpsmembers and the taxpayers who foot the bill. Not surprisingly, program participants reap most of the benefits from the Job Corps. However, taxpayers also gain from reduced social program and criminal justice costs, and from the labor value of the projects corpsmembers contribute while enrolled. Overall, the cost-benefit ratio for taxpayers is only slightly negative, 98 cents for every dollar invested.

Although benefits persisted during the four-year follow-up period, the analysts assumed that the benefits of the Job Corps diminished after time. However, if the benefits continue throughout

Table 6.8.

Corpsmembers trained as clerks achieve the best long-term labor market success compared with a control group.

	Increased earnings (1977 dollars)
Average	$ 655
Men	
General or sales clerk	1251
Welder	1186
Electrician	1150
Carpenter	695
Auto repair	605
Mason	546
Cook or baker	242
Custodial or maintenance	235
Painter	-651
Women	
General or sales clerk	1708
Clerk typist or secretary	495
Nurse's or medical assistant	189

Source: Mathematica Policy Research, Inc.

former enrollees' working lives, the program's cost-benefit ratio would be much more favorable, $2.11 for every dollar invested — over $10,000 per corpsmember in 1986 dollars.[30]

Although the evaluation of the Job Corps reviewed the experiences of enrollees who entered the program a decade ago, there is no reason to believe the corps is less effective today. In fact, the current program is probably more effective because the proportion of early dropouts has declined and average training duration has increased.

A Quarter Century of Progress

Despite some anxious moments, the Job Corps has survived the Reagan administration attacks relatively unscathed. Nonetheless, staff cuts at the federal level and reduced resources for research and development threaten the corps' ability to experiment with new approaches to serve severely disadvantaged youth. Contrary to fashionable deprecations of Washington, the Job Corps' achievements are due both to national leadership as well as the dedicated center staff which the program has consistently attracted. Since its inception, the Job Corps has collected the information necessary to pinpoint problems and taken steps to enhance its educational, vocational, and residential programs. Other JTPA components could benefit greatly by adopting these practices.

Efforts to boost training quality and provide a greater proportion of enrollees with high school equivalency degrees are now underway. Additional funding would permit expanded use of computers in instruction, which showed considerable promise in a late 1970s study. However, given the program's high costs, efforts to improve cost efficiency should also continue. Increasing individual center capacity would undoubtedly reduce unit costs. While reductions are possible, as long as the Job Corps operates residential facilities it will remain an expensive program, albeit cost-effective in the long run.

7
Farmworker and
Indian Programs

In addition to the Job Corps, Congress retained federal administration over programs for two special groups who are among the poorest members of American society: migrant and seasonal farmworkers and Indians. Even the Reagan administration acknowledged that the migration patterns of many farmworkers make state administration inadvisable, and efforts to aid Native Americans have traditionally been the responsibility of the federal government.

Migrant and Seasonal Farmworkers

The conclusions of the latest presidential commission which examined the problems of migrant and seasonal farm laborers in 1978 remain valid today.

> American farmworkers and their families still live and work under conditions which are cruel and harsh by any standard: They are ill-housed, ill-clothed, under-nourished, face enormous health hazards, are underpaid, underemployed, undereducated, socially isolated, politically powerless, excluded from much of the work-protective legislation that other American workers take for granted, and unable to compete in the labor market for the higher wages that would permit them to resolve their own problems or ameliorate the bleak reality of their existence.[1]

Given the nature of their employment, involving geographic mobility or intermittent work, estimates of the number of migrant and seasonal farmworkers are necessarily subject to significant

159

variations. After a drastic decline throughout most of this century, the overall hired farmworker population appears to have stabilized at roughly 1.5 million in the 1980s. The most disadvantaged of these are the approximately 250,000 migrant farmworkers, and the poor seasonal farmworkers whose number is uncertain.[2] Because of the low pay, temporary employment and difficult working conditions, migrant and seasonal farm labor is dominated by poor immigrants, many from Mexico, who often face even harsher working conditions in their native country.

Federal farmworker employment and training programs date back to the 1964 Economic Opportunity Act, and were incorporated into CETA with a separate earmarked appropriation. Except for the introduction of performance standards, JTPA made no significant changes in the program's statutory authority.

Financing

Congress stipulated that annual JTPA farmworker appropriations equal 3.2 percent of Title IIA funding, although actual appropriations have sometimes slightly exceeded this amount, as follows:

	Appropriation
Oct. 1983-June 1984	$45.3 million
1984	65.5
1985	60.4
1986	57.8
1987	59.6
1988 (proposed)	57.1

In inflation-adjusted dollars, the 1987 appropriation was a third of CETA's 1980 funding level. Farmworker programs operate in 48 states and Puerto Rico, but nearly two-fifths of the funds are allocated to California, Texas, Florida, Puerto Rico and North Carolina.

Most projects are administered by community-based organizations initially established by the antipoverty programs of the 1960s. All participating grantees operate statewide projects, except in California. Six training contractors administer 23 of the 53 total projects, and receive 41 percent of all funds. The average project received slightly over $1 million from JTPA in 1986, distributed as follows:

Allocation	Distribution by Number of projects	Distribution by Funding received
Total	53	96.1%
Under $500,000	15	6.4
$500,000 - $999,999	16	21.3
$1 million - $1,999,999	17	39.2
$2 million - $2,999,999	2	9.9
Over $3 million	3	19.3

The Labor Department reserves approximately 4 percent of the annual appropriation, primarily for farmworker housing assistance.

A 1986 analysis sponsored by the Labor Department's inspector general concluded that the financial management records of farmworker projects were inadequate to ensure that funds were properly spent, and that the Labor Department had done little to correct previously identified problems. Many of the grantees had not been audited in three years. However, most of the problems uncovered were resolved, and the inspector general recommended disallowing less than 1 percent of total expenditures.[3]

Enrollees and Services

JTPA assists some 50,000 farmworkers annually, less than half the number served by CETA. Individuals who (1) did a minimum of 25 days of farm work or earned $400 in farm wages in any consecutive 12-month period in the previous two years, (2) obtain at least half of their earnings or spend half of their time engaged in farm work and (3) belong to an impoverished family are eligible for assistance. The average enrollee earned less than $3000 in the year before entering JTPA, and nearly two-fifths had eight years of schooling or less. Despite their destitution, few farmworker enrollees receive welfare. Enrollees are about equally divided between migrant and seasonal farmworkers (table 7.1).

Table 7.1
The typical JTPA farmworker enrollee is a minority adult male
with less than a high school education.

	JTPA (1985)	CETA (1979-81 average)
Total	50,054	123,800
Migrant	47%	55%
Seasonal	53	45
Male	64	63
Female	36	37
Hispanic	56	54
Black	21	26
White	20	17
Other	3	3
16-21	23	33
22-44	62	49
Over 44	15	18
High school dropout	68	67
High school student	1	14
High school graduate	31	19
Limited English	27	27
Welfare recipient	11	NA
Single parent	12	NA

Source: U.S. Department of Labor, Employment and Training Administration

Over three-fourths of program funds are devoted to training, but less than half of the enrollees receive any training. The majority receive nontraining services, costing an average of $124 in 1985. These services are targeted at migrant enrollees, and include health care, meals, temporary shelter, child care and transportation (table 7.2). Enrollees receiving some form of training remain in the program for an average of five months. Most classroom training probably emphasizes basic education skills, because less than a third of farmworker grantees offer occupationally-specific classroom training. One analyst concluded that occupational classroom training is of satisfactory quality, based on teacher qualifications, training duration, and the views of former participants and the employers who hired them.[4] Other "training assistance" — a catchall category including job search training, counseling, and outreach and eligibility determination costs — is the least expensive training-related assistance.

Table 7.2
About half of JTPA farmworker enrollees receive services only (1985).

	Terminees	Costs	Total nonadministrative costs per terminee	Support service costs per terminee
Total	41,824	$64.2 million	$1252	$133
Nontraining services only	53%	4%	124	124
Classroom training	19	40	3189	196
On-the-job training	15	20	2005	88
Training assistance	8	8	1459	95
Work experience	4	9	3842	244
Administration	-	18	-	-

Source: U.S. Department of Labor, Employment and Training Administration

Expenditures for support services have declined sharply since the late 1970s, when CETA allocated over a third of its farmworker program budget to support assistance. Emphasizing training, the Labor Department limited nontraining-related support services to 15 percent of a local project's budget. As in other programs under JTPA, OJT and job search assistance have increased compared to CETA, and the funding of work experience projects has declined.

Outcomes

The Labor Department has issued performance standards governing expected job placement rates and costs per placement. However, the department has relied too heavily upon these measures to guide the program and paid too little attention to the quality of training that enrollees receive.

For 1986, projects were expected to match 1984 performance results within a fairly generous 15 percentage point margin, but the adjustment margin could not lower the job placement standard below a 40 percent rate or raise average costs per placement above $8,000. Participants receiving services only are excluded from the calculations for the standards, and administrative costs are not considered in assessing costs per placement.

For JTPA's first three years, farmworker performance standards did not credit youth positive terminations, as did the Title IIA program. Consequently, youth enrollees who learned the 3Rs were counted as negative terminations, which discouraged remedial education programs and increased costs per placement. Although beginning in July 1986 youth positive terminations were no longer considered a negative outcome, the performance system still does not encourage provision of remedial education for youth.

Outcomes for JTPA's first three years follow:

	Oct. 1983- June 1984	1984	1985
Job placement rate	66%	62%	62%
Cost per placement	$3556	$4044	$4543
including administrative costs	$4472	$4974	$5548

Anecdotal reports indicate that projects manipulate enrollment and termination data to attain prescribed standards. Labor Department auditors found that about 5 percent of reported JTPA placements could not be verified.[5]

Reported job placement rates are comparable with the Title IIA program, as is the average hourly wage of $4.58. Costs per placement are nearly $2000 higher, probably because training duration is longer in the farmworker program. JTPA farmworker program performance cannot be directly compared with CETA, which did not report results separately for trainees and those receiving support services only. Counting all terminees, CETA job placement rates during 1982-3 were about 20 percent, compared to 29 percent for JTPA in 1985. However, since CETA provided a larger proportion of enrollees with services only, JTPA and CETA placement results probably do not differ significantly. CETA terminees who found work earned slightly over $4 hourly, about the same as JTPA terminees after adjusting for wage growth.

Most job placements are for nonagricultural jobs. About half of those who find work do so in occupations unrelated to their training. Job holders generally earn higher hourly wages than they did in their previous employment.[6] White enrollees have the best placement results, while those with limited English language skills are least successful at finding work (table 7.3). High school dropouts attained a relatively high 59 percent placement rate, but not surprisingly fared worse than graduates. Seasonal farmworkers have much higher placement rates than migrants.

Table 7.3.
White male high school graduates are most successful at finding employment (1985).

Characteristic	Placement Rate
Total	62%
Migrant	52
Seasonal	65
Male	66
Female	57
Hispanic	59
Black	55
White	74
16-21	61
22-44	64
Over 44	56
High school dropout	59
High school graduate	67
Limited English	47
Welfare recipient	56
Single parent	55

Source: U.S. Department of Labor, Employment and Training Administration

Work experience and classroom training have the highest reported costs per placement, over twice as expensive as OJT or training assistance, although significant miscategorization distorts the accuracy of these comparisons. OJT placement rates are significantly higher than other forms of training.

Service	Placement rate	Cost per placement
Total	62%	$4543
Classroom training	53	5987
On-the-job training	80	2507
Training assistance	53	2756
Work experience	60	6388

Despite its costliness, effective classroom training, by improving participants' education and skills, may achieve the most durable employability gains.

Follow-up surveys of former enrollees and their employers indicate a need for greater Labor Department attention to local operations. Many employers with OJT contracts said they would have hired the workers without a subsidy. Eighteen percent of the placements were for temporary jobs, and 13 percent for part-time work. A large proportion of individuals who are placed remain with the same employer for only a short time (about half are let go), although most subsequently find work.[7] These deficiencies reflect the difficulties involved in assisting poor farmworkers as well as program inadequacies. In some cases a temporary or part-time placement may represent the best alternative. Nevertheless, the findings reinforce the necessity for increased Labor Department oversight and federal funding to provide more intensive training.

The JTPA farmworker program is seriously overextended in attempting to stretch insufficient funds to serve its client population. By increasing the number of immigrant farmworkers with legal status in this country, the new immigration law has expanded the eligible population and placed an even greater burden on the program.

Native Americans

Indian families living on or near reservations have average incomes only two-fifths as large as the typical American family, but must stretch this income to raise an average of twice as many children.[8] The Indian unemployment rate estimated by the U.S. Bureau of Indian Affairs approaches 50 percent.[9] Because of their extreme poverty and joblessness, Indians were early beneficiaries of federal employment and training assistance and antipoverty programs, but no separate Indian training program existed until the enactment of CETA. Except for the introduction of performance standards, JTPA made no significant changes in the program's statutory authority.

Funding

Congress stipulated that annual JTPA Indian appropriations equal 3.3 percent of Title IIA funding, although actual appropriations have sometimes slightly exceeded this amount.

	Appropriation
Oct. 1983 - June 1984	$46.7 million
1984	62.2
1985	62.2
1986	59.6
1987	61.5
1988 (proposed)	58.8

Indian grantees in selected areas also share in the distribution of summer youth employment funds, and received $13.6 million in 1987. Largely because of the elimination of CETA public service jobs, Indian employment and training funds have drastically decreased since the 1979 peak appropriation of $222 million, over four times larger in inflation-adjusted dollars than JTPA's 1987 funding. Cuts in related Indian social programs compounded problems caused by diminished employment and training assistance.

Indian programs operate in all states, but Arizona, California and Oklahoma, where nearly two-fifths of the Indian population reside, receive an identical proportion of the funds. For 1987, 190 grantees — including tribal governments, intertribal consortia, and off-reservation Indian organizations — received an average of about $325,000 to administer the program, but the average masked an incredible degree of diversity (figure 7.1). The plethora of small programs is due to the dispersion of small groups of Indians throughout the United States, funding cuts since CETA, and a governmental decision to maintain separate administrative authority for smaller tribes and bands. To maximize administrative efficiency, some tribes consolidate JTPA and other federal program funds. The Labor Department recommended disallowing 5 percent of the expenditures audited between October 1983 and March 1987, a rate significantly higher than the other federally administered training programs.[10] However, historically most costs recommended for disallowance have been approved on appeal.

Figure 7.1
Relatively few projects receive most JTPA Indian funds (1987).

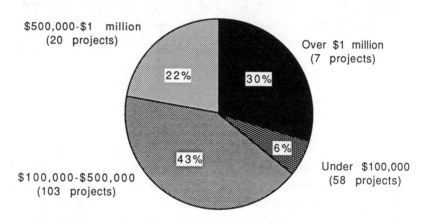

$500,000-$1 million (20 projects)

22%

30%

Over $1 million (7 projects)

43%

6%

$100,000-$500,000 (103 projects)

Under $100,000 (58 projects)

Source: U.S. Department of Labor, Employment and Training Administration

Enrollees and Services

Federal regulations permit assistance to nearly any Native American who is unemployed, underemployed or economically disadvantaged, making several hundred thousand Indians eligible for JTPA. Some 54,000 Indians enrolled in various JTPA programs in 1985, as follows:

Native American programs (Title IV)	32,700
Summer youth programs (Title IIB)	12,000
Adult and youth programs (Title IIA)	6,000
Job Corps	2,500
Dislocated worker programs	1,000

Because the number of eligible Indians far exceeds available JTPA slots, local Indian program administrators adopt a variety of screening mechanisms with widely divergent goals. The typical JTPA Title IV Indian enrollee is an adult high school graduate who earned less than $4000 in the year before entering JTPA. Characteristics of the Indians enrolled during 1985 follow:

Male	51%
Female	49
14-15	2
16-21	28
22-44	63
Over 44	7
High school dropout	27
High school student	8
High school graduate	65
Welfare recipient	22
Single parent	18

Classroom training, subsidized public employment, and job search assistance account for most of the aid received by JTPA Indian program participants, who, on average, remain enrolled for a little over 3.5 months (table 7.4). Reported data should be regarded as, at best, ballpark estimates. Data collection has measurably improved since CETA, when Labor Department records were extremely spotty. Major reporting deficiencies continue, however, due to misunderstanding of reporting terms or deliberate misreporting of performance outcomes and the Labor Department's inadequate monitoring and technical assistance.

Table 7.4
Unlike other JTPA programs, subsidized public employment remains an important part of the Indian program (1985).

	Participants	Costs	Nonadministrative costs per participant
Total	32,700	$61.4 million	$1492
Classroom training	31%	17%	1065
Work experience	22	19	1669
On-the-job training	10	6	1185
Public service employment	7	12	3450
Training assistance	{31	20	{1489
Services only		5	
Administration	-	21	-

Source: U.S. Department of Labor, Employment and Training Administration

Nearly a third of participants receive classroom vocational training. Projects utilize community colleges and private vocational schools where available, allowing enrollees a broad selection of occupational choices, but classroom training programs on isolated reservations are usually limited to secretarial or construction trades.

Unlike other JTPA programs, the use of subsidized public employment — including public service employment and work experience — remains important in Indian programs, accounting for nearly a third of participant enrollment. Because Indians face extremely high unemployment and have limited access to jobs on the reservation, Congress stipulated that the Labor Department could not prohibit local administrators from operating public service employment programs. This did not prevent the Labor Department from attempting to limit public jobs spending to 10 percent of a grantee's allocation or to the official unemployment rate percentage, whichever is higher, but local programs have countered by reclassifying public service employment as work experience. Enrollees in subsidized positions primarily perform clerical work for tribal enterprises and social programs. With 25-40 applicants per opening due to severe job shortages on reservations, competition for these slots is often severe.

As in the farmworker program, "training assistance" is a catchall category including job search assistance, counseling, and outreach and eligibility costs. These programs, which typically offer no more than a few days of assistance, have significantly increased since CETA despite the limited usefulness of job search programs in areas where few job openings exist.

On-the-job training remains limited due to insufficient private jobs on reservations and persistent bias against Indians off reservations. Nonreservation OJT participants have more varied vocational options, although most tend to work in fast food restaurants, gas stations, and entry level jobs in offices. OJT slots on reservations are generally restricted to construction trades.[11]

Outcomes

The Labor Department has issued JTPA Indian program performance standards governing expected job placement and positive termination rates as well as costs per positive termination. The positive termination standards reflect an important goal, but are too ambiguously defined to adequately assess performance. Reported outcomes indicate an improvement compared to CETA's final year.

	1983 (CETA)	Oct. 1983- June 1984	1984	1985
Job placement rate	33%	49%	47%	47%
Positive termination rate	66%	80%	80%	79%
Cost per positive termination	$3003	$2642	$2294	$2250

Trainees who found work earned an average of $4.97 hourly. Since few public service employment and work experience enrollees find unsubsidized work, these two programs have high costs per entered employment, as follows:

Service	Cost per placement
Average	$ 4,922
Classroom training	4,041
Work experience	8,537
On-the-job training	2,127
Public service employment	15,047
Training assistance and services only	2,469

The Labor Department's overreliance on performance standards for reservations illustrates the department's inflexible dedication to quantifying results. Before 1987, each project faced standards based on its performance in prior years, but the Labor Department then implemented standards based on a regression model similar to that used in the Title IIA program. Local operators have vigorously protested the model's suitability for Indian reservations, as the Labor Department's action flies in the face of the well-established fact that reservation economic and demographic data are unreliable. In the absence of reservation-specific data, the local economic factors incorporated in the model use data for the surrounding county, which may contain a relatively large non-Indian population. Another problem is that since over half of Indian programs have fewer than 100 terminees per year, minor differences in enrollee characteristics from year to year can cause significant shifts in performance targets.[12]

Federal employment and training programs have played an important albeit insufficient role in improving the labor market prospects of Indians. It would be unrealistic to expect that meager employment funds could invigorate the depressed economies of most reservations. Nonetheless, funding cuts and lackluster federal administration have impaired the effectiveness of JTPA Indian programs. The Labor Department's misguided single-minded emphasis on performance standards and neglect of more substantive oversight has engendered much friction between the department and local administrators, to the detriment of the program.[13]

8

Taking Stock

The Job Training Partnership Act has garnered broad political support for employment assistance in aid of the unskilled and deficiently educated poor. Business representatives and conservatives — including President Reagan — who heaped abuse upon CETA, now sing JTPA's praises. The importance of a positive image should not be underestimated: for all of CETA's achievements, its unpopularity doomed the program. Nonetheless, JTPA's accomplishments fall short of the claims of the Reagan administration and many program administrators.

The Last Should Be First

JTPA has stressed training and downgraded support services as well as income support. But the quality of training and the selection of trainees for the limited available slots have received little attention. To attain "success," local programs have tended to exclude the functional illiterates JTPA was presumably meant to serve. Consideration of applicants' income, employment history and educational attainment should be an integral part of the training program. *To effectively implement the law, the Labor Department should require local projects to utilize these criteria as well as reading and math skill tests to screen in rather than screen out those most in need of JTPA services.* Teaching these individuals the 3Rs should be a priority because basic literacy is a prerequisite to gain access to and satisfactorily perform on even entry-level jobs.

JTPA's strict limitations on stipends and support services prevent poor individuals from enrolling in or completing training programs.

173

An assessment of support needs should be an integral part of each new enrollee's employability development plan. Local staff should ascertain whether lack of child care, health care, or transportation would inhibit the successful completion of training. *To enable localities to provide essential services, Congress should liberalize the 15 percent limit on support service expenditures to allow stipends on a broader basis, scaled to the income and financial resources of the enrollee's family, and the Labor Department should promote increased use of stipends and services.* As in the Job Corps, stipends should also reward participants who complete training courses. Dismissing individuals who make little progress or demonstrate insufficient effort would discourage those looking for a handout.

In the absence of careful oversight, contractors may cut corners on training quality to increase profits or in response to federal or local pressures to reduce costs. Unless enrollees acquire skills which are valued in the marketplace, JTPA is unlikely to achieve more than fleeting gains in enhancing the employability of the poor. The quality of remedial education and occupational training can be improved by providing localities with the funds to hire better qualified instructors, purchase necessary equipment, and operate programs of sufficient length. *Job Corps curricula should be tested at selected localities and adapted as necessary to enhance the quality of education and training in other JTPA components.* Local programs should exercise greater care in negotiating on-the-job training contracts to avoid subsidizing employers for hiring individuals they would have engaged without government inducements.

Federal standards for admissions and training quality require substantial technical assistance and monitoring to ensure effective implementation. New regulations will in turn necessitate significant alterations in performance standards, which currently encourage both creaming and brief training courses. Without efforts to verify the accuracy of reported results, contractors can exaggerate, fudge or even falsify their reports with impunity. Thus the performance outcomes, which proclaim JTPA's exemplary record, are based on data of questionable reliability. *The Labor Department should at least perform spot-check audits of reported contractor performance.* Without uniform, enforced federal standards for program content, competency-based standards discourage localities from offering quality programs because superficial courses produce the best results on paper at minimal costs. Meaningful competency benchmarks should be applicable to deficiently educated adults as well as youth. To assist schools and local training programs to reach those in need and to help them attain basic educational competency, the federal government could fund private organizations that would establish networks for implementing the basic competency goals.[1] *Achievement of a high school equivalency diploma should be the goal for enrollees who have not completed their secondary education.* Finally, to reflect the fact that performance standards are far less scientifically-derived than the Labor Department pretends, the targets should be expressed as a range of acceptable performance rather than a specific number.

Despite congressional emphasis on basic education, JTPA's summer youth employment program remains primarily a work experience activity. Amendments requiring that a fourth of the funds be spent on basic education failed to gain congressional approval in 1986, but the principle remains sound. While providing job opportunities may be necessary to entice disadvantaged youth to enroll in a summer educational program, work experience alone — especially the payment of the hourly minimum wage to 14- and 15-year-olds — is not the best investment of three-quarters of a billion dollars annually. Localities should also have the authority to use summer program funds to serve youth in year-round training programs.

Congress is currently considering President Reagan's proposed increase in dislocated worker funding together with an expanded federal role in administration. States have feebly managed the program and left a third of allocated funds unspent, leaving thousands of displaced workers without assistance. Specialized permanent personnel at the local level to plan and implement timely responses to major layoffs and plant closings would be costly and not feasible. *The Labor Department should assemble teams of experts to help states and localities organize dislocated worker projects as soon as notice of prospective layoffs becomes available.* However, even the most efficient dislocated worker project will be handicapped by the failure of firms to provide sufficient warning of mass layoffs. At present, only half of even large corporations provide any advance notice of mass layoffs to workers, and in these cases the average length of notice is only a month and a half. *Excluding special circumstances, Congress should require large firms to provide three months advance notice of major layoffs and plant closings.*

The exemplary accomplishments of the Job Corps have been recognized across the political spectrum. However, personnel reductions during the 1980s have seriously hampered the Labor Department's ability to monitor and maintain program standards, let alone improve operations. Audits have demonstrated a particular need to verify results reported by placement agencies.

The seemingly intractable poverty of migrant farmworkers and reservation Indians necessitates far more resources and energetic efforts than currently provided by JTPA. The Labor Department should provide more intensive technical assistance and experiment with new approaches for these hard to serve groups. The department has funded only one evaluation of the Indian and farmworker programs in more than a decade. Without more thorough research, departmental efforts to improve the programs will not provide optimal returns on the federal investment.

Minding the Store

JTPA's designers assumed that delegating oversight to the states would produce better management and more effective results. However, in four years of operations, few states have demonstrated initiative in administering JTPA, and most are content to follow the minimum requirements of the law. Even the Reagan administration — by proposing a new dislocated worker program with an expanded federal role — has tacitly acknowledged that state management of JTPA's Title III is wanting.

Improving JTPA's operations does not require altering its administrative structure. In fact, such a realignment would impede necessary reforms. Congress has historically devoted too much attention to details dealing with the division of administrative responsibility, at the expense of emphasizing and overseeing program quality. Dynamic federal action would require few statutory changes, but would necessitate a renewed sense of mission by the

Labor Department. Although the federal government was castigated for allegedly stifling local creativity during CETA, the
extraordinary diversity of local programs belied this allegation. *A
more vigorous federal role will not hamper states which are dedicated
to improving JTPA's performance.*

Congressional financial support and constructive oversight are
critical to undergird increased federal direction of JTPA. Deficit
concerns made Congress all too acquiescent to the administration's
sharp curtailment of Employment and Training Administration
staff. *Effective monitoring and technical assistance, as well as greater
accountability for program expenditures, are not possible without
more federal personnel.* Because states have provided remarkably
little support for technical assistance, and because the provision of
assistance by 50 different states is inherently inefficient, funds
dedicated to technical assistance and incentive awards for superior
SDA performance (the 6 percent set-aside) should be reallocated to
the Labor Department. This will not prevent the department from
reimbursing states that provide useful technical assistance.

Equal congressional attention should be devoted to prodding the
Labor Department to more energetically monitor JTPA activities.
Following the law's enactment, states and localities expected and
sought federal direction and guidance in implementing the new
program, but the administration shunned its responsibilities. Congress has also remained largely a passive observer of the program's
evolution, intervening only to block administration efforts to cut
JTPA's budget and to enact minor amendments in 1986. Oversight
hearings have been generally superficial, and even the Labor
Department's failure to submit required annual reports prompted
no response from Congress. A Congress content to follow the path
of least resistance will likely cave in to state and local objections to
stricter federal guidance, even when the complaints are driven by no
more than turf jealousies or bureaucratic resistance to change.

JTPA stresses the coordination of job training efforts with related
social programs, but experience has shown that states and localities
have made little progress since the law's enactment. Moreover,
SDA administrators are small cogs in the wheels of government,
lacking the leverage necessary to influence other programs. Closer
cooperation would undoubtedly enhance JTPA's effectiveness, but

it cannot mitigate the effects of drastically reduced budgets. A broad brush approach to coordination will probably remain ineffective. *JTPA should instead integrate coordination efforts into projects designed to achieve specific ends.* For example, increased utilization of the community college system would confer mainstream credentials on poor individuals who successfully complete courses. The Labor Department should carefully select attainable coordination goals and work closely with states and localities to specify the objectives, define the obstacles, and carefully evaluate the success or failure of different approaches.

Congress should simplify the 8 percent education set-aside and eliminate the 3 percent older worker set-aside. The former should remain under state direction, but Congress should restrict its use to remedial education and abolish the remaining statutory provisions, which complicate administration of the funds. The older worker program also unnecessarily complicates administration, and the money could be used more efficiently by permitting the Senior Community Service Employment Program to operate training programs.

The effects of increasing the role of business in JTPA require close scrutiny. Although business has played an important part in enhancing the legitimacy of job training programs and giving SDAs access to additional community resources, private industry council business members too frequently demonstrate a shortsighted attachment to "bottom line" performance indicators which may poorly reflect the actual effectiveness of JTPA in the long run. Revised federal standards and constant monitoring are necessary to insure that SDAs pursue federal priorities.

Knowledge is Valuable

Policy shapers and program administrators need operational data to run programs effectively. *The federal government should significantly enhance data collection as well as research efforts at all three levels of government.* The following information, subject to uniform federal definitions, should be collected for each enrollee:

- participant characteristics (including entry reading and math attainment as well as employment and earnings history;

- receipt of training, support services and stipends;
- duration (in hours) and the dollar value of each service;
- educational and occupational achievements in the program;
- reason for termination; and
- postprogram occupational and educational attainments.

To reduce administrative costs and facilitate analysis of the data collected, as well as to disseminate the findings, Congress should provide funds for compatible computer systems, at least at the state level.

If properly executed, the experiment now underway to determine JTPA's effectiveness may represent an improvement over previous Labor Department evaluations of employment and training programs. However, the random assignment of individuals to either training or control groups will be extremely difficult to implement successfully, particularly in the case of on-the-job training programs. Therefore, these experiments should be considered an adjunct to, rather than a substitute for, other methods of evaluating JTPA. *The Labor Department should reconsider its decision to cancel the Census Bureau's longitudinal survey, which was designed to provide information about the long-term experiences of former participants.*

It Can't Be Done With Mirrors

Job training programs have unquestionably enhanced the employability of the poor, but they cannot do the job alone. Without a sound educational system, enough jobs, adequate wages and strict enforcement of antidiscrimination laws, JTPA cannot be fully effective. During CETA, job creation received at least as much attention as training, but Congress could not overcome the Reagan administration's adamant opposition to a permanent public service employment program even when unemployment reached nearly 11 percent. In mid-1987, during the fifth year of the economic recovery, a monthly average of 7.3 million Americans who sought work were unable to find it. In one of four states, the unemployment rate exceeded 8 percent, a level historically associated with a recession. *Public service employment projects, even if not restricted to the poor, would expand total employment and thereby make it easier for the disadvantaged to find work.*

Improving training quality, targeting the most disadvantaged clientele, expanding the use of stipends, and providing public service jobs will increase the costs but also the effectiveness of JTPA. Reliance on creaming and brief job search programs produces superficial and fleeting gains. The lasting results of the Job Corps' more intensive instruction suggest that JTPA's reliance on brief training will not meet the goals Congress established for the program.

Despite persistent budget deficits, Congress appears willing to consider increases in funding for employment and training programs. Opinion polls also indicate that nearly three of four Americans regard support of education and training as the best means to combat poverty.[2] However, new budget authority for training welfare recipients may mean a further fragmentation of service delivery. *It is far more appropriate to boost JTPA funds than to create separate training programs for the welfare and the nonwelfare poor, categorizations which have little meaning outside the minds of policymakers.*

Only a small fraction of the employable poor are served by JTPA. Even if Congress raised appropriations to the 1981 level, employment and training assistance would represent less than two-thirds of 1978 outlays. Without additional funds, JTPA cannot hope to have more than a marginal impact. The proposal to increase employment and training assistance by nearly $6 billion annually involves a return to the 1981 appropriations level — an approximate doubling of current funding (table 8.1). To reap optimum benefits and to avoid the administrative difficulties which plagued CETA, the expansion should be phased in gradually. This recommended increase, while still woefully inadequate in terms of unmet needs, will be difficult to enact given present federal budget deficits. However, continuing national concern over the problems of dislocated workers, welfare recipients, and the deficiently educated may facilitate budget increases for employment and training programs.

The largest proposed increase, over $3 billion, would boost funds for

occupational training and basic education. The funds would be
divided among various JTPA training components and the adult
education program. The 1987 budget currently permits assistance to
no more than about 1 in 20 eligible persons. Increased funding
would permit more intensive programs, reaping enhanced long-
term benefits. Work incentive (WIN) funding should be maintained,
but incorporated into Title IIA year-round training programs to
bolster administrative cost efficiency. Enforcement responsibility
for WIN's nontraining functions (e.g., job search requirements)
would remain a state responsibility. Providing remedial education
to a fourth of the summer program's teenage enrollees would cost
an additional $100 million annually.

*The second largest proposed increase would be for job creation to
ameliorate job shortages which have persisted even during the prolonged economic recovery following the two most recent recessions. A*

Table 8.1
**Substantial increases in employment and training funds are necessary
to meet the needs of the poor and unemployed (millions).**

Program		1987	Recommended increase	Total
Total		$5077	$5959	$11,036
JTPA		3656	3159	6815
Title IIA	Adult and youth programs	1840	1900	3740
Title IIB	Summer youth programs	750	100	850
Title III	Dislocated worker programs	200	800	1000
Title IV	Federally administered programs			
	Job Corps	656	200	856
	Native American program	62	38	100
	Migrant and seasonal farmworker programs	60	40	100
	Technical assistance, research and pilot projects	79	81	160
Related programs		1421	2800	4221
Public service employment		-	2500	2500
Employment service		778	100	878
Senior community service employment program		326	-	326
Work incentive program (1986)		211	-	211
Adult education		106	200	306

Source: Congressional appropriations

$2.5 billion annual appropriation would create about 250,000 job slots. Another $100 million would be devoted to the employment service or other state-designated agencies to help these public workers and other poor individuals find unsubsidized jobs.

Greater funding and federal direction will render JTPA more effective, but the task is fraught with difficulties. Ironically, JTPA's claimed outstanding performance will impede reforms of the system's shortcomings. Making the present standards more rigorous and requiring program operators to serve a more disadvantaged clientele will likely erode the reported success record, giving the appearance that JTPA is deteriorating and fostering potential political and public relations problems. Short-sighted policies have led JTPA into a blind alley, and at present it is difficult to see an easy way out.

Appendices

A. EMPLOYMENT AND TRAINING ABCs

AFDC	Aid to Families with Dependent Children
BLS	U.S. Bureau of Labor Statistics
CETA	Comprehensive Employment and Training Act
CBO	Community-based organization
CCC	Civilian conservation center (Job Corps)
ETA	Employment and Training Administration (Department of Labor)
GAO	U.S. General Accounting Office
GED	General education development test
JTPA	Job Training Partnership Act
Title IIA	Year-round training programs for adults and youth
Title IIB	Summer youth employment and training programs
Title III	Dislocated worker programs
MDTA	Manpower Development and Training Act
OJT	On-the-job training
PIC	Private industry council
RA	Resident adviser (Job Corps)
SDA	Service delivery area
SER	Service, employment and redevelopment program
TAA	Trade adjustment assistance
TJTC	Targeted jobs tax credit
UI	Unemployment insurance
WIN	Work incentive program
YEDPA	Youth Employment and Demonstration Projects Act

B. QUESTIONNAIRE FOR STATE ADMINISTRATORS

1. *Targeted assistance.* How did the state implement JTPA's requirements that programs serve a) individuals "most in need," b) dropouts, and c) welfare recipients?

   Please provide written state policy related to these requirements.

2. *Underspending.* Has the state issued any regulations which encourage SDAs to fully expend their job training allocation? Does the state collect data on the proportion of SDA funds *obligated* within a given program year?

   If so, please attach reports.

3. *Services.* Did the state require SDAs to implement competency programs? If so, were *educational* competency programs specifically required? Were standards issued detailing the content of the educational programs?

   Please attach policy directives.

4. *Sanctions.* Has the state issued policy directives on sanctions for
       a) violations of the law, or
       b) failure to meet performance standards?

   Please attach policy directives.

5. *Data collection.* Did the state add to or modify federal data collection requirements? Specifically, did the state require SDAs to:
       a) Distinguish between part-time vs. full-time, or permanent vs. temporary jobs?
       b) Collect information on the number of *hours* participants spent in the program?
       c) Collect cost data by program activity?
       d) Utilize a standard definition for enrollment in or termination from JTPA?

QUESTIONNAIRE FOR SDAs

Federal Role

1. How has federal administration of JTPA changed since Brock and Semerad assumed their offices? Are the feds more responsive to state and local inquiries? If yes, has this affected SDA operations in any significant way?
2. If you thought that the feds would be responsive, what assistance would you seek from them?

States

1. What program priorities has the state established?
2. Is 6 percent incentive money influential in determining state or local priorities?
3. Have state interventions improved or impeded local programs? How are SDA activities constrained by state law or regulations?
4. Has the state rejected or modified any local biennial plans? On what grounds? How were conflicts resolved?
5. Did your state appropriate any direct funds to supplement federal allocations? Please indicate the amount of state supplements for:
     Title II A
     Title II B
     Title III
     Any other part of JTPA
     Any program related to JTPA (specify)
6. Please attach copies of state follow-up reports regarding employment status and wages of former JTPA enrollees.

Local Programs

1. Comparing JTPA with CETA, is the PIC/LEO partnership administratively preferable to the prime sponsor system? Why or why not?

2. Selection of clients:
   a. To what extent do performance standards determine program choices and selection of participants? What other factors are important?
   b. What criteria are used to screen applicants?
   c. What educational or other tests are given?
   d. During program year 1985, what proportion of eligible applicants are turned away?

   Number _____

   Percentage _____

   e. Are service providers represented on PICs? Do they influence PIC decisions? Do service providers who are not represented influence JTPA planning and services? How?

3. Do federal requirements determine the local data collection system? What additional information is collected? What part do the data play in subsequent program decisions? Please attach state or local evaluations of SDAs.

4. Please attach copies of the local biennial plan.

5. What proportion of SDA funds has been allocated to local workfare efforts?

   Amount _____

   Percentage _____

6. Did the state JTPA administrators audit SDAs? What dollar amount of expenditures has been disallowed or questioned? Why?

7. Please provide the following information:

	Adults			Youth		
	Cost Per Placement	Duration Of Training		Cost Per Placement	Duration of Training	
		Wks.	Hrs.		Wks.	Hrs.
a. All programs						
b. Classroom training						
c. OJT						
d. Job search						
e. Work experience						
f. Basic education						
g. Other (specify)						

8. What percentage of SDA training funds is allocated to each of the following entities:

	Amount	Percentage
Public post-secondary institutions	_____	_____
Public high schools	_____	_____
Community-based organizations	_____	_____
Private vocational schools	_____	_____
Employment service	_____	_____
The SDA's administrative agency	_____	_____
Other (specify)	_____	_____

9. What entity is primarily responsible for
   a. Outreach and recruitment
   b. Eligibility determinations

If more than one entity provides these services, please indicate how the funds are proportionately allocated to each.

10. What proportion of terminees receive placement assistance from the following entities:

	Number	Percentage
Total terminees	_____	_____
SDAs administrative agency	_____	_____
Employment service	_____	_____
Community-based organizations	_____	_____
Training contractor (excluding the above)	_____	_____
Other (specify)	_____	_____

11. What proportion of funds for training is allocated through performance based contracts?

Amount _____ Percentage _____

12. What proportion of the SDA's allocation is devoted to allowances?

Amount _____ Percentage _____

What is the average weekly payment for participants receiving allowances?

13. What proportion of enrollees receive remedial or basic education:

	Number	Percentage
Adults		
Youth		

14. What were the three leading occupations enrollees were trained for?

15. Please attach copies of reports on the post-program experiences of JTPA participants.

Future

1. What amendments to JTPA, if any, would you recommend to Congress?

2. Would you want to add a job creation component to JTPA? If yes, how large? If not, why?

Notes

1. A Continued Federal Commitment

1 U.S. Bureau of Labor Statistics, *Linking Employment Problems to Economic Status* (Washington: U.S. Government Printing Office, 1987), forthcoming.

2 Herbert S. Parnes, *Unemployment Experience of Individuals Over a Decade* (Kalamazoo, Michigan: W.E. Upjohn Institute for Employment Research, 1982), pp. 14, 34; Richard B. Freeman, "Troubled Workers in the Labor Market," in National Commission for Employment Policy, *Seventh Annual Report: The Federal Interest in Employment and Training* (Washington: National Commission for Employment Policy, October 1981), p. 115.

3 U.S. Department of Education, "Update on Adult Illiteracy," 1986 (mimeo); Richard L. Venezky, Carl F. Kaestle, and Andrew M. Sum, *The Subtle Danger* (Princeton, New Jersey: Educational Testing Service, January 1987).

4 Anne McDougall Young, "One-Fourth of the Adult Labor Force Are College Graduates," *Monthly Labor Review,* February 1985, p. 43; and U.S. Bureau of the Census, *Money Income of Households, Families, and Persons in the United States: 1984* (Washington: U.S. Government Printing Office, April 1986), Current Population Reports, Series P-60, No. 151, Table 33, pp. 126-32.

5 Francis W. Horvath, "The Pulse of Economic Change: Displaced Workers of 1981-85," *Monthly Labor Review,* June 1987, pp. 3-12; U.S. Bureau of Labor Statistics, *Displaced Workers, 1979-83* (Washington: Government Printing Office, July 1985), Bulletin 2240, p. 21.

6 U.S. Bureau of the Census, *Characteristics of the Population Below the Poverty Level: 1984* (Washington: U.S. Government Printing Office, June 1986), Current Population Reports, Series P-60, No. 152, Table 8, pp. 28-30 and *Money Income of Households, Families, and Persons in the United States: 1984* (Washington: U.S. Government Printing Office, April 1986), Current Population Reports, Series P-60, No. 151, Table 33, pp. 126-32; unpublished U.S. Bureau of Labor Statistics data.

189

7 This section is adapted from Sar A. Levitan and Garth L. Mangum, "A Quarter Century of Employment and Training Policy: Where Do We Go From Here?," in *Jobs for the Future* (Washington: Center for National Policy, May 1984), pp. 40-42. Background works on employment and training programs before JTPA include Sar A. Levitan and Garth L. Mangum, *Federal Training and Work Programs in the Sixties* (Ann Arbor, Michigan: Institute of Labor and Industrial Relations, 1969); Garth L. Mangum, *A Decade of Manpower Development and Training* (Salt Lake City, Utah: Olympus Publishing Company, 1973); Ewan Clague and Leo Kramer, *Manpower Policies and Programs* (Kalamazoo, Michigan: W.E. Upjohn Institute for Employment Research, 1976); Robert Taggart, *A Fisherman's Guide* (Kalamazoo, Michigan: W.E. Upjohn Institute for Employment Research, 1981); Sar A. Levitan and Garth L. Mangum (eds.), *The T in CETA* (Kalamazoo, Michigan: W.E. Upjohn Institute for Employment Research, 1981); William Mirengoff, Lester Rindler, Harry Greenspan and Charles Harris, *CETA* (Kalamazoo, Michigan: W.E. Upjohn Institute for Employment Research, 1982); Andrew Hahn and Robert Lerman, *What Works in Youth Employment Policy?* (Washington: National Planning Association, 1984); Grace A. Franklin and Randall B. Ripley, *CETA* (Knoxville, Tennessee: The University of Tennessee Press, 1984); Donald C. Baumer and Carl E. Van Horn, *The Politics of Unemployment* (Washington: Congressional Quarterly Press, 1985); Charles L. Betsey, Robinson G. Hollister, Jr., and Mary R. Papageorgiou (eds.), *Youth Employment and Training Programs* (Washington: National Academy Press, 1985); and Robert F. Cook, Charles F. Adams, Jr., V. Lane Rawlins and Associates, *Public Service Employment* (Kalamazoo, Michigan: W.E. Upjohn Institute for Employment Research, 1985).

8 U.S. General Accounting Office, *Implementation of the Phaseout of CETA Public Service Jobs* (Washington: GAO, April 14, 1982), HRD-82-48, p. 6.

9 Patricia W. McNeil, "The Job Training Partnership Act: A Chronology of its Development with Recommendations for the Future," prepared for the House Committee on Education and Labor, 1987 (forthcoming), chapters 2 and 3 present a discussion of JTPA's legislative history.

10 Robert Taggart, *A Fisherman's Guide* (Kalamazoo, Michigan, W.E. Upjohn Institute for Employment Research, 1981), p. vii.

2. The Reluctant Partners:
Program Management

[1] Neal R. Peirce and Robert Guskind, "Job Training for Hard-Core Unemployed Continues to Elude the Government," *National Journal*, September 28, 1985, p. 2197.

[2] U.S. General Accounting Office, *Concerns Within the Job Training Community Over Labor's Ability to Implement the Job Training Partnership Act* (Washington: GAO, April 22, 1985), HRD-85-61, pp. 3-5, 8-10.

[3] Review by the authors of selected 1986 compliance reviews.

[4] Abt Associates Inc., *An Assessment of Funding Allocation Under the Job Training Partnership Act* (Cambridge, Massachusetts: Abt Associates Inc., August 31, 1986), pp. 32, 42, 103.

[5] Demetra Smith Nightingale, *Federal Employment and Training Policy Changes During the Reagan Administration: State and Local Responses* (Washington: The Urban Institute, May 1985), pp. 29-32.

[6] National Job Training Partnership, Inc., "Funding Cuts, Shifts Hit Over 70 Percent of JTPA Service Delivery Areas, Partnership Survey Shows," *Washington Update Supplement*, No. 161, April 23, 1986.

[7] U.S. General Accounting Office, *Concerns Within the Job Training Community Over Labor's Ability to Implement the Job Training Partnership Act* (Washington: GAO, April 22, 1985), HRD-85-61, pp. 11-12; Testimony of Roberts Jones, Deputy Assistant Secretary of ETA, in U.S. Congress, House Committee on Education and Labor, Subcommittee on Employment Opportunities, *Oversight Hearing on the Implementation of the Job Training Partnership Act* (Washington: Government Printing Office, October 10, 1985), Serial No. 99-54, p. 27.

[8] General Accounting Office, *Strong Leadership Needed to Improve Management at the Department of Labor* (Washington: GAO, October 21, 1985), HRD-86-12, pp. 86-95.

[9] "Brock Sets Lofty Tone for New 'ETA' Era at 'NAB' Annual Convention," *Employment and Training Reporter* (Washington: Bureau of National Affairs, October 9, 1985), p. 130.

[10] William J. Gainer, U.S. General Accounting Office, in U.S. Congress, Senate Committee on Labor and Human Resources, Subcommittee on Employment and Productivity, *Job Training Partnership Act Amendments of 1986* (Washington: Government Printing Office, March 11, 1986), S. Hrg. 99-681, p. 125.

[11] Abt Associates Inc., *Measuring the Costs of JTPA Program Participation* (Cambridge, Massachusetts: Abt Associates Inc., September 30, 1984), pp. 126, 155.

[12] U.S. General Accounting Office, *Job Training Partnership Act: Data Collection Efforts and Needs* (Washington: GAO, March 1986), HRD-86-69BR, pp. 18-23.

[13] Grinker Associates, Inc., *An Independent Sector Assessment of the Job Training Partnership Act* (New York: Grinker Associates, Inc., July 1986); Westat, Inc., *Implementation of the Job Training Partnership Act: Final Report* (Rockville, Maryland: Westat, Inc., November 1985).

[14] Response to authors' questionnaire.

[15] Response to authors' questionnaire.

[16] Westat, Inc., *Implementation of the Job Training Partnership Act: Final Report* (Rockville, Maryland: Westat, Inc., November 1985), pp. 2:2-3, 11-13.

[17] Westat, Inc., *Implementation of the Job Training Partnership Act: Final Report* (Rockville, Maryland: Westat, Inc., November 1985), pp. 4:4-6.

[18] National Alliance of Business, *Is the Job Training Partnership Working?* (Washington: NAB, 1986), p. 37.

[19] Congressional Budget Office, *The Federal Role in State Industrial Development Programs* (Washington: CBO, July 1984), p. 37.

[20] Edward F. Dement, *Final Report: State Job Training Coordinating Councils* (Washington: National Commission for Employment Policy, May 1985), RR-85-11, pp. 2-4; Rodney Riffel, *Job Training: A Legislator's Guide* (Washington: National Conference of State Legislatures, September 1986), pp. 18, 41, 52.

[21] Response to authors' questionnaire.

[22] Westat, Inc., *State Level Implementation of the Job Training Partnership Act* (Rockville, Maryland: Westat, Inc., May 16, 1984), pp. 2:10, 3:6-8; National Alliance of Business, *An Overview of the New Job Training System* (Washington: NAB, January 1984), p. 2.

[23] Response to authors' questionnaire.

[24] National Governors' Association and National Alliance of Business, *Report on Joint Survey of State Provision of JTPA Technical Assistance* (Washington: NGA, April 1985), p. 2 and Table III.

[25] Gary Walker, Hilary Feldstein and Katherine Solow, *An Independent Sector Assessment of the Job Training Partnership Act* (Washington: National Com-

mission for Employment Policy, January 1985), p. 80; National Governors' Association, *Assessment of Adult and Youth Performance Standards Under the Job Training Partnership Act* (Washington: National Commission for Employment Policy, November 1985), RR-85-13, pp. 11, 13.

[26] Response to authors' questionnaire.

[27] U.S. General Accounting Office, *Job Training Partnership Act: Initial Implementation of Program for Disadvantaged Youth and Adults* (Washington: GAO, March 4, 1985), HRD-85-4, pp. 56-7 (updated).

[28] National Alliance of Business, *What's Happening With JTPA?* (Washington: NAB, 1985), p. 7.

[29] National Alliance of Business, *What's Happening with JTPA?* (Washington: NAB, 1985), pp. 34-5; *An Overview of the New Job Training System* (Washington: NAB, January 1984), p. 9; and *Is the Job Training Partnership Working?* (Washington: NAB, 1986), pp. 20, 30-1.

[30] Grinker Associates, Inc., *An Independent Sector Assessment of the Job Training Partnership Act: Final Report* (New York: Grinker Associates, Inc., July 1986), pp. 62, 83-4, 87-9.

[31] National Alliance of Business, *Is the Job Training Partnership Working?* (Washington: NAB, 1986), pp. 10-13, 41-4, and *What's Happening with JTPA?* (Washington: NAB, 1985), pp. 36-7.

[32] Grinker Associates, Inc., *An Independent Sector Assessment of the Job Training Partnership Act: Final Report* (New York: Grinker Associates, Inc., July 1986), pp. 101-3.

[33] National Alliance of Business, *Is the Job Training Partnership Working?* (Washington: NAB, 1986), pp. 27-9, 47-9.

[34] National Alliance of Business, *Is the Job Training Partnership Working?* (Washington: NAB, 1986), pp. 16-17, and *What's Happening with JTPA?* (Washington: NAB, 1985), p. 5.

[35] Responses to authors' questionnaire.

[36] Westat, Inc., *Implementation of the Job Training Partnership Act: Final Report* (Rockville, Maryland: Westat, Inc., November 1985), pp. 4:14-15, 19-20; Gary Walker, Hilary Feldstein and Katherine Solow, *An Independent Sector Assessment of the Job Training Partnership Act* (Washington: National Commission for Employment Policy, January 1985), p. 52; Grinker Associates, Inc., *An Independent Sector Assessment of the Job Training Partnership Act: Final Report* (New York: Grinker Associates, Inc., July 1986), pp. 92-100; and National Alliance of Business, *Is the Job Training Partnership Working?* (Washington: NAB, 1986), p. 33.

[37] William R. Barnes and R. Leo Penne, *Employment Problems and America's Cities* (Washington: National League of Cities, 1984), p. A-13.

[38] Grinker Associates, Inc., *An Independent Sector Assessment of the Job Training Partnership Act* (New York: Grinker Associates, Inc., July 1986), pp. 93-4; Westat, Inc., *Transition Year Implementation of the Job Training Partnership Act* (Rockville, Maryland: Westat, Inc., January 1985), pp. 4:21-5.

[39] William Mirengoff, Lester Rindler, Harry Greenspan and Charles Harris, *CETA: Accomplishments, Problems, Solutions* (Kalamazoo, Michigan: W.E. Upjohn Institute for Employment Research, 1982), pp. 97-8, 289-90.

[40] Edward F. Dement, *Final Report: State Job Training Coordinating Councils* (Washington: National Commission for Employment Policy, May 1985), RR-85-11, pp. 19-20.

[41] Macro Systems, Inc., *Assessment of the Implementation and Effects of the JTPA Title V Wagner-Peyser Amendments* (Silver Spring, Maryland: Macro Systems, Inc., December 1985), pp. 5:27-30 and Exhibit V-8, 3:3, 5, 13, 15, 27, 39; MDC, Inc., *Trends in ES/JTPA Coordination, PY 1984-1986* (Washington: Interstate Conference of Employment Security Agencies, 1987), pp. 12, Appendix 1, p. 2.

[42] Macro Systems, Inc., *Assessment of the Implementation and Effects of the JTPA Title V Wagner-Peyser Amendments* (Silver Spring, Maryland: Macro Systems, Inc., December 1985), pp. 4:6-7, 14, 5:17, 6:20, 22.

[43] Interstate Conference of Employment Security Agencies, Inc., *JTPA and the Employment Service: The First Year* (Washington: ICESA, 1985); National Alliance of Business, *What's Happening with JTPA?* (Washington: NAB, 1985), p. 18.

[44] Gregory Wurzburg and Joseph Coleman, *Involving Schools in Employment and Training Programs for Youth* (Washington: National Council on Employment Policy, May 1979), pp. 29-30; Charles L. Betsey, Robinson G. Hollister, Jr., and Mary R. Papageorgiou (eds.), *Youth Employment and Training Programs* (Washington: National Academy Press, 1985), p. 85.

[45] U.S. Department of Education, *The Vocational Education Study: The Final Report* (Washington: U.S. Department of Education, September 1981), Vocational Education Study Publication No. 8, p. 5:26.

[46] Edward F. Dement, *Final Report: State Job Training Coordinating Councils* (Washington: National Commission for Employment Policy, May 1985), RR-85-11, p. 17; Westat, Inc., *Implementation of the Job Training Partnership Act: Final Report* (Rockville, Maryland: Westat, Inc., November 1985), p. 2:25.

[47] Fernando L. Alegria, Jr. and Jose R. Figueroa, *Study of the JTPA Eight Percent Education Coordination and Grants Set-Aside and the Three Percent Set-Aside*

Training Program for Older Individuals (Washington: National Governors' Association, March 1986), pp. 24, 28-31.

48 Lawrence Neil Bailis, *Study of the Status of FY 83 CETA Coordination and Program Activities: Final Report* (Washington: National Commission for Employment Policy, May 1984), RR-84-05, p. 36.

49 Jose R. Figueroa, *Bridges to Self-Sufficiency: A Study of Work and Welfare Programs and Their Linkages with the Employment and Training System* (Washington: National Governors' Association, July 1986), p. 19.

50 Lawrence Neil Bailis, *Study of the Status of PY 85 JTPA Coordination and PY 84 Program Activities* (Washington: National Commission for Employment Policy, June 1986), pp. 2:12-13 (draft).

51 Senator Dan Quayle, "Report on Oversight of the Job Training Partnership Act in Indiana," *Congressional Record* (daily edition), October 1, 1985, p. S 12391.

52 Fernando L. Alegria, Jr. and Jose R. Figueroa, *Study of the JTPA Eight Percent Education Coordination and Grants Set-Aside and the Three Percent Set-Aside for Older Individuals* (Washington: National Governors' Association, March 1986), pp. 6-9, 11-18.

53 Westat, Inc., *Implementation of the Job Training Partnership Act: Final Report* (Rockville, Maryland: Westat, Inc., November 1985), p. 4:11; Lawrence Neil Bailis, *The More Things Change...* (Washington: National Commission for Employment Policy, March 1987), RR-87-25, p. 44.

54 Kris M. Balderston, *Inventory of State Actions to Coordinate State Programs and Policies: State Employment, Training and Economic Development Linkage Project* (Washington: National Governors' Association, September 1985), pp. 3, 15.

3. Training Adults and Youth

1 Grinker Associates, Inc., *An Independent Sector Assessment of the Job Training Partnership Act: Final Report* (New York: Grinker Associates, Inc., July 1986), p. 62.

2 Westat, Inc., *Implementation of the Job Training Partnership Act: Final Report* (Rockville, Maryland : Westat, Inc., November 1985), pp. 5:20-3; responses to authors' questionnaire.

3 Congressional Budget Office, *Work-Related Programs for Welfare Recipients* (Washington: CBO, April 1987), p. 19.

4 Karen Blumenthal, "Job-Training Effort, Critics Say, Fails Many Who Need Help Most," *Wall Street Journal*, February 9, 1987, p. 1.

[5] Gary Orfield and Helene Slessarev, *Job Training Under the New Federalism* (Chicago: University of Chicago, 1986), p. 173.

[6] Gary Walker, Hilary Feldstein and Katherine Solow, *An Independent Sector Assessment of the Job Training Partnership Act* (Washington: National Commission for Employment Policy, January 1985), pp. 32-3; Craig Mellow, "Motown's Manpower Renewal," *Across the Board*, June 1987, p. 36.

[7] U.S. General Accounting Office, *The Job Training Partnership Act: An Analysis of Support Cost Limits and Participant Characteristics* (Washington: GAO, November 6, 1985), HRD-86-16, p. 10.

[8] William Mirengoff, Lester Rindler, Harry Greenspan and Charles Harris, *CETA: Accomplishments, Problems, Solutions* (Kalamazoo, Michigan: W.E. Upjohn Institute for Employment Research, 1982), pp. 144-6.

[9] Judith M. Gueron, *Work Initiatives for Welfare Recipients* (New York: Manpower Demonstration Research Corporation, March 1986), p. 21.

[10] National Alliance of Business, *Is the Job Training Partnership Working?* (Washington: NAB, 1986), pp. 57-8; U.S. General Accounting Office, *Job Training Partnership Act: Initial Implementation of Program for Disadvantaged Youth and Adults* (Washington: GAO, March 4, 1985), HRD-85-4, p. 32.

[11] Westat, Inc., *AFDC Recipients in JTPA* (Rockville, Maryland: Westat, Inc., July 1986), pp. 9-10 (draft).

[12] Howard S. Bloom, *The Effect of Eliminating Allowances From CETA Training Programs: Final Report* (Washington: National Commission for Employment Policy, May 1985), RR-85-03, pp. 1, 30.

[13] Robert Taggart, *A Fisherman's Guide* (Kalamazoo, Michigan: W.E. Upjohn Institute for Employment Research, 1981), pp. 316-17.

[14] National Alliance of Business, *What's Happening with JTPA?* (Washington: NAB, 1985) p. 17.

[15] U.S. General Accounting Office, *The Job Training Partnership Act: An Analysis of Support Cost Limits and Participant Characteristics* (Washington: GAO, November 6, 1985), HRD-86-16, pp. 15-17.

[16] Response to authors' questionnaire.

[17] U.S. General Accounting Office, *The Job Training Partnership Act: An Analysis of Support Cost Limits and Participant Characteristics* (Washington: GAO, November 6, 1985), HRD-86-16, pp. 17, 20-1, 22-5, 28-30; Gary Orfield and Helene Slessarev, *Job Training Under the New Federalism* (Chicago: University of Chicago, 1986), p. 221.

[18] Westat, Inc., *Implementation of the Job Training Partnership Act: Final Report* (Rockville, Maryland: Westat, Inc., November 1985), pp. 6:31-2.

[19] Robert Taggart, "A Review of CETA Training," in Sar A. Levitan and Garth L. Mangum (eds.), *The T in CETA* (Kalamazoo, Michigan: W.E. Upjohn Institute for Employment Research, 1981), p. 128.

[20] Westat, Inc., *Implementation of the Job Training Partnership Act: Final Report* (Rockville, Maryland: Westat, Inc., November 1985), p. 6:17; Lawrence Neil Bailis, *The More Things Change...* (Washington: National Commission for Employment Policy, March 1987), RR-87-25, pp. 14, 22, 24.

[21] Westat, Inc., *Transition Year Implementation of the Job Training Partnership Act* (Rockville, Maryland: Westat, Inc., January 1985), p. 7:13; Lawrence Neil Bailis, *The More Things Change...* (Washington: National Commission for Employment Policy, March 1987), RR-87-25, pp. 16, 25.

[22] U.S. Congressional Budget Office and National Commission for Employment Policy, *CETA Training Programs — Do They Work for Adults?* (Washington: CBO, July 1982), p. A-42; Karen Blumenthal, "Job-Training Effort, Critics Say, Fails Many Who Need Help Most," *Wall Street Journal,* February 9, 1987, p. 1.

[23] John Bishop (ed.), *Subsidizing On-the-Job Training* (Columbus, Ohio: National Center for Research in Vocational Education, September 1982), pp. 12-13.

[24] Westat, Inc., *Implementation of the Job Training Partnership Act: Final Report* (Rockville, Maryland: Westat, Inc., November 1985), p. 6:23; Sar A. Levitan and Frank Gallo, "The Targeted Jobs Tax Credit," *Labor Law Journal,* October 1987, pp. 641-9.

[25] Westat, Inc., *Implementation of the Job Training Partnership Act: Final Report* (Rockville, Maryland: Westat, Inc., November 1985), pp. 6:8-9, 21, 31-2.

[26] Gordon Berlin, Andrew Sum and Robert Taggart, "Cutting Through," paper presented to the Ford Foundation Welfare State Committee, December 1986.

[27] U.S. General Accounting Office, *Youth Job Training: Problems Measuring Attainment of Employment Competencies* (Washington: GAO, February 1987), pp. 17-18, 22, 27, 34.

[28] Macro Systems, Inc., *Study of the FY 1983 Summer Youth Employment Program* (Silver Spring, Maryland: Macro Systems, Inc., January 31, 1984).

[29] Sar A. Levitan and Frank Gallo, "The Targeted Jobs Tax Credit," *Labor Law Journal,* October 1987, pp. 641-9.

[30] Human Environment Center, "Conservation and Service Corps Profiles," November 1986, pp. 5-7.

[31] Abt Associates, Inc., *An Assessment of Funding Allocation Under the Job Training Partnership Act* (Cambridge, Massachusetts: Abt Associates, Inc., August 31, 1986), pp. 32, 59, 103.

[32] Macro Systems, Inc., *Study of the FY 1983 Summer Youth Employment Program* (Silver Spring, Maryland: Macro Systems, Inc., January 31, 1984), pp. 2:7, 11-14, 23, 48-50.

[33] Macro Systems, Inc., *Study of the FY 1983 Summer Youth Employment Program* (Silver Spring, Maryland: Macro Systems, Inc., January 31, 1984), pp. 2:1-2, 4-7, 9, 15, 17, 34-8.

[34] National Job Training Partnership, Inc., *Education in Local JTPA Summer Youth Programs* (Washington: NJTP, Inc., August 25, 1986), pp. 5, A-3-4, B-1-3; U.S. Department of Labor, Employment and Training Administration, "Fiscal Year 1982 Program Status and Financial Summary," QPR No. 1-83, January 31, 1983, p. 1115.

[35] U.S. General Accounting Office, *Job Training Partnership Act: Summer Youth Programs Increase Emphasis on Education* (Washington: GAO, June 1987), HRD-87-101BR, pp. 3, 13, 16, 18, 22.

[36] Natalie Jaffe, *Summer Employment Programs for Disadvantaged Youth: Issues and Options* (Philadelphia: Public/Private Ventures, July 1985), p. 7.

[37] Cynthia L. Sipe, Jean Baldwin Grossman and Julita A. Milliner, *Summer Training and Education Program (STEP): Report on the 1986 Experience* (Philadelphia: Public/Private Ventures, April 1987), pp. vii-ix, 156, 163-6.

[38] Macro Systems, Inc., *Study of the FY 1983 Summer Youth Employment Program* (Silver Spring, Maryland: Macro Systems, Inc., January 31, 1984), pp. 2:10-11.

[39] Grinker Associates, Inc., *An Independent Sector Assessment of the Job Training Partnership Act: Final Report* (New York: Grinker Associates, Inc., July 1986), p. 89; Gary Orfield and Helene Slessarev, *Job Training Under the New Federalism* (Chicago: University of Chicago, 1986), p. 177.

[40] U.S. General Accounting Office, *Labor Should Make Sure CETA Programs Have Effective Employability Development Systems* (Washington: GAO, January 13, 1982), HRD-82-2, pp. 28, 31, 33; William Mirengoff, Lester Rindler, Harry Greenspan and Charles Harris, *CETA: Accomplishments, Problems, Solutions* (Kalamazoo, Michigan: W.E. Upjohn Institute for Employment Research, 1982), pp. 144, 175-6.

[41] National Alliance of Business, *Is the Job Training Partnership Working?* (Washington: NAB, 1986), p. 55.

[42] Katherine Solow, *The Job Training Partnership Act: Service to Women* (New York: Grinker, Walker & Associates, 1986), pp. 19, 29; Wisconsin Department of Industry, Labor and Human Relations, Division of Employment and Training Policy, *Services to Women in Wisconsin's Major Employment and Training Programs,* August 1986, pp. 27-8; Abby Spero, *Is the Job Training Partnership Act Training Displaced Homemakers?* (Washington: Displaced Homemakers Network, October 1985), pp. 4, 6.

[43] National Alliance of Business, *Is the Job Training Partnership Working?* (Washington: NAB, 1986), p. 22, and *What's Happening with JTPA?* (Washington: NAB, 1985), pp. 11-12.

[44] Gary Walker, Hilary Feldstein and Katherine Solow, *An Independent Sector Assessment of the Job Training Partnership Act* (Washington: National Commission for Employment Policy, January 1985), pp. 26-7.

[45] National Alliance of Business, *What's Happening with JTPA?* (Washington: NAB, 1985), pp. 10-14.

[46] Demetra Smith Nightingale and Carolyn Taylor O'Brien, *Community Based Organizations in the Job Training Partnership System* (Washington: The Urban Institute, October 1984), pp. 24-28, 38, 40-3.

[47] Sar A. Levitan and Garth L. Mangum (eds.), *The T in CETA* (Kalamazoo Michigan: W.E. Upjohn Institute for Employment Research, 1981), pp. 40-1.

[48] "Community-Based Organizations Wrestle with JTPA Limitations," *Employment and Training Reporter* (Washington: Bureau of National Affairs, June 13, 1984), p. 1057.

[49] National Alliance of Business, *What's Happening with JTPA?* (Washington: NAB, 1985), pp. 12-13.

[50] Gary Walker, Hilary Feldstein and Katherine Solow, *An Independent Sector Assessment of the Job Training Partnership Act* (Washington: National Commission for Employment Policy, January 1985), pp. 22-3; Gary Orfield and Helene Slessarev, *Job Training Under the New Federalism* (Chicago: University of Chicago, 1986), p. 243.

[51] Lawrence Neil Bailis, *The More Things Change...* (Washington: National Commission for Employment Policy, March 1987), RR-87-25, p. 29; Westat, Inc., *Implementation of the Job Training Partnership Act: Final Report* (Rockville, Maryland: Westat, Inc., November 1985), pp. 8:22-6.

[52] Response to authors' questionnaire.

4. Performance Standards and Results

[1] Grace A. Franklin and Randall B. Ripley, *CETA: Politics and Policy, 1973-1982* (Knoxville: University of Tennessee Press, 1984), pp. 174-7.

[2] National Commission on Employment and Unemployment Statistics, *Counting the Labor Force* (Washington: Government Printing Office, 1979), pp. 253-263.

[3] U.S. General Accounting Office, *Youth Job Training: Problems Measuring Attainment of Employment Competencies* (Washington: GAO, February 1987), p. 47.

[4] SRI International, *Development of Adjustment Models for PY 86 Performance Standards, Final Report* (Menlo Park, California: SRI International, June 1986), p. 3:18.

[5] Westat, Inc., *Implementation of the Job Training Partnership Act: Final Report* (Rockville, Maryland: Westat, Inc., November 1985), pp. 8:5-6; Grinker Associates, Inc., *An Independent Sector Assessment of the Job Training Partnership Act: Final Report* (New York: Grinker Associates, Inc., July 1986), pp. 106-7; and Brandeis University Center for Human Resources and the National Association of Private Industry Councils, "Performance Standards: A Report from the Field," *Youth Programs,* Summer 1986, p. 8.

[6] National Governors' Association, *Assessment of Adult and Youth Performance Standards Under the Job Training Partnership Act* (Washington: National Commission for Employment Policy, November 1985), RR-85-13, p. 35.

[7] Westat, Inc., *Implementation of the Job Training Partnership Act: Final Report* (Rockville, Maryland: Westat, Inc., November 1985), p. 8:11.

[8] National Governors' Association, *Assessment of Adult and Youth Performance Standards Under the Job Training Partnership Act* (Washington: National Commission for Employment Policy, November 1985), RR-85-11, pp. 13, 15-23.

[9] National Alliance of Business, *Is the Job Training Partnership Working?* (Washington: NAB, 1986), p. 63.

[10] Post-program surveys by Georgia, Massachusetts, North Dakota, Texas, and Vermont.

[11] Gary Orfield and Helene Slessarev, *Job Training Under the New Federalism* (Chicago: University of Chicago, 1986), p. 190.

[12] Karen Blumenthal, "Job-Training Effort, Critics Say, Fails Many Who Need Help Most," *Wall Street Journal,* February 9, 1987, p. 1; Westat, Inc., *Implementation of the Job Training Partnership Act: Final Report* (Rockville, Maryland: Westat, Inc., November 1985), pp. 6:4-5, 7-8.

[13] Karlyn Barker, "Trainees' Hard Road to Learning a Trade," *Washington Post,* December 1, 1986, p. 1.

[14] U.S. General Accounting Office, *Many Proprietary Schools Do Not Comply with Department of Education's Pell Grant Program Requirements* (Washington: GAO, August 20, 1984), HRD-84-17, pp. 16-17.

[15] Massachusetts Office of Training and Employment Policy, "Post-Program Performance of JTPA Participants," July 1986, p. 6; Georgia Department of Labor, Memorandum from Assistant Commissioner H.G. Weisman, "Participant Follow-Up Monthly Report," September 10, 1986, p. 5.

16 Charles L. Betsey, Robinson G. Hollister, Jr., and Mary R. Papageorgiou (eds.), *Youth Employment and Training Programs: The YEDPA Years* (Washington: National Academy Press, 1985), pp. 137-74; Judith M. Gueron, *Work Initiatives for Welfare Recipients* (New York: Manpower Demonstration Research Corporation, March 1986), pp. 15, 17; Manpower Demonstration Research Corporation, *Summary and Findings of the National Supported Work Demonstration* (Cambridge, Massachusetts: Ballinger Publishing Company, 1980), pp. 5-9.

17 Westat, Inc., *Continuous Longitudinal Manpower Survey Follow-Up Report No. 13* (Rockville, Maryland: Westat, Inc., December 1984), p. 7:9.

18 "Jones Searches for Policy Mid-Ground in 'Mau-Mau' Talk with JTPA Managers," *Employment and Training Reporter* (Washington: Bureau of National Affairs, October 10, 1984), p. 127.

19 Robert Taggart, "A Review of CETA Training," in Sar A. Levitan and Garth L. Mangum (eds.), *The T in CETA* (Kalamazoo, Michigan: W.E. Upjohn Institute for Employment Research, 1981), p. 103.

20 Westat, Inc., *Continuous Longitudinal Manpower Survey Follow-Up Report No. 13* (Rockville, Maryland: Westat, Inc., December 1984), p. 6:2, Appendix Table D-32.

21 Congressional Budget Office and the National Commission for Employment Policy, *CETA Training Programs — Do They Work for Adults?* (Washington: CBO, July 1982), pp. A-6-7.

22 "Symposium on the Econometric Evaluation of Manpower Training Programs," *The Journal of Human Resources,* Spring 1987, pp. 154-5.

23 Indiana Office of Occupational Development, *The Return on Investment from Indiana's Training Programs Funded Through the Job Training Partnership Act,* October 31, 1986, pp. 8-9.

24 Vermont Department of Employment and Training, "PY'87 JTPA Follow-Up Survey", undated, pp. 7-8.

25 Response to author's questionnaire.

26 U.S. General Accounting Office, *CETA Programs for Disadvantaged Adults — What Do We Know About Their Enrollees, Services, and Effectiveness?* (Washington: GAO, June 14, 1982), IPE-82-2, p. 30.

5. Aiding Dislocated Workers

[1] Charles F. Stone and Isabel V. Sawhill, *Labor Market Implications of the Growing Internationalization of the U.S. Economy* (Washington: National Commission for Employment Policy, June 1986), RR-86-20, p. 21.

[2] Congressional Budget Office, *Dislocated Workers: Issues and Federal Options* (Washington: U.S. Government Printing Office, July 1982), p. ix.

[3] Francis W. Horvath, "The Pulse of Economic Change: Displaced Workers of 1981-85," *Monthly Labor Review,* June 1987, pp. 3-12.

[4] Abt Associates Inc., *Final Report: Defense Industrial Worker Assistance Programs* (Cambridge, Massachusetts: Abt Associates, Inc., May 10, 1985), pp. 36, Exhibit 4.5.

[5] U.S. House of Representatives, Committee on Ways and Means, *Background Material and Data on Programs Within the Jurisdiction of the Committee on Ways and Means* (Washington: U.S. Government Printing Office, March 6, 1987), WMCP:100-4, pp. 318, 320; U.S. Office of Technology Assessment, *Trade Adjustment Assistance: New Ideas for an Old Program* (Washington: U.S. Government Printing Office, June 1987), OTA-ITE-346, p. 25.

[6] Robert Guttman, "Reflections on Title III," in William H. Kolberg (ed.), *The Dislocated Worker* (Washington: Seven Locks Press, 1983), p. 61.

[7] Francis W. Horvath, "The Pulse of Economic Change: Displaced Workers of 1981-85," *Monthly Labor Review,* June 1987, p. 6.

[8] William Gainer, U.S. General Accounting Office, in U.S. Congress, House Committee on Education and Labor, Subcommittee on Employment Opportunities, *Oversight Hearing on the Job Training Partnership Act (Part 3)* (Washington: U.S. Government Printing Office, November 8, 1985), Serial No. 99-41, p. 21.

[9] U.S. General Accounting Office, *Dislocated Workers: Local Programs and Outcomes Under the Job Training Partnership Act* (Washington: GAO, March 1987), HRD-87-41, pp. 87-8.

[10] U.S. Office of Technology Assessment, *Plant Closing: Advance Notice and Rapid Response* (Washington: U.S. Government Printing Office, September 1986), OTA-ITE-321, p. 31.

[11] Kris M. Balderston, *Plant Closings, Layoffs, and Worker Readjustment: The States' Response to Economic Change* (Washington: National Governors' Association, July 1986), p. 9.

[12] Westat, Inc., *Implementation of the Job Training Partnership Act: Final Report* (Rockville, Maryland: Westat, Inc., November 1985), pp. 9:17-19.

[13] U.S. Office of Technology Assessment, *Technology and Structural Unemployment: Reemploying Displaced Adults* (Washington: U.S. Government Printing Office, February 1986), OTA-ITE-250, p. 195; U.S. General Accounting Office, *Dislocated Workers: Local Programs and Outcomes Under the Job Training Partnership Act* (Washington: GAO, March 1987), HRD-87-41, pp. 24-6.

[14] CSR, Inc., *Study of Selected Aspects of Dislocated Worker Programs: Final Report* (Washington: CSR, Inc., April 1986), p. 59.

[15] U.S. Office of Technology Assessment, *Plant Closing: Advance Notice and Rapid Response* (Washington: U.S. Government Printing Office, September 1986), OTA-ITE-321, p. 29.

[16] Westat, Inc., *Implementation of the Job Training Partnership Act: Final Report* (Rockville, Maryland: Westat, Inc., November 1985), pp. 10:27-28.

[17] U.S. Office of *Technology Assessment, Technology and Structural Unemployment: Reemploying Displaced Adults* (Washington: U.S. Government Printing Office, February 1986), OTA-ITE-250, p. 190.

[18] Robert Cook (ed.), *Worker Dislocation* (Kalamazoo, Michigan: W.E. Upjohn Institute for Employment Research, 1987), U.S. General Accounting Office, *Dislocated Workers: Extent of Business Closures, Layoffs, and the Public and Private Response* (Washington: GAO, July 1986), HRD-86-116BR, pp. 9, 22-5; and *Dislocated Workers: Local Programs and Outcomes Under the Job Training Partnership Act* (Washington: GAO, March 1987), HRD-87-41, pp. 14, 28-9, 84.

[19] Lawrence Neil Bailis, *The More Things Change...* (Washington: National Commission for Employment Policy, March 1987), RR-87-25, pp. 35, 37.

[20] U.S. Office of Technology Assessment, *Trade Adjustment Assistance: New Ideas for an Old Program* (Washington: U.S. Government Printing Office, June 1987), OTA-ITE-346, pp. 9-10.

[21] U.S. General Accounting Office, *Dislocated Workers: Local Programs and Outcomes Under the Job Training Partnership Act* (Washington: GAO, March 1987), HRD-87-41, pp. 80, 89.

[22] CSR, Inc., *Intake Systems for Dislocated Worker Programs: Matching Dislocated Workers to Appropriate Services* (Washington: CSR, Inc., February 1986), pp. 2-5, 14, 30.

[23] U.S. General Accounting Office, *Dislocated Workers: Extent of Business Closures, Layoffs, and the Public and Private Response* (Washington: GAO, July 1986), HRD-86-116BR, pp. 23.

[24] U.S. General Accounting Office, *Dislocated Workers: Local Programs and Outcomes Under the Job Training Partnership Act* (Washington: GAO, March 1987), HRD-87-41, pp. 46-7.

[25] CSR, Inc., *Operating Effective Reemployment Strategies for Dislocated Workers* (Washington: CSR, Inc., March 1986), pp. 2-6, 9, 11, 29, and *Intake Systems for Dislocated Workers: Matching Dislocated Workers to Appropriate Services* (Washington: CSR, Inc., February 1986), pp. 4-5.

[26] U.S. General Accounting Office, *Dislocated Workers: Local Programs and Outcomes Under the Job Training Partnership Act* (Washington: GAO, March 1987), HRD-87-41 pp. 47-50, 80.

[27] U.S. Office of Technology Assessment, *Technology and Structural Unemployment: Reemploying Displaced Adults* (Washington: U.S. Government Printing Office, February 1986), OTA-ITE-250, p. 185.

[28] CSR, Inc., *Operating Effective Reemployment Strategies for Dislocated Workers* (Washington: CSR, Inc., March 1986), pp. 3-4, 10-11.

[29] Westat, Inc., *Issues for Active State Management of the JTPA Title III Grant* (Rockville, Maryland: Westat, Inc., April 28, 1986), pp. 1-2; National Alliance of Business, *What's Happening with JTPA?* (Washington: NAB, 1985), p. 26.

[30] William Gainer, U.S. General Accounting Office, in U.S. Congress, House Committee on Education and Labor, Subcommittee on Employment Opportunities, *Oversight Hearing on the Job Training Partnership Act (Part 3)* (Washington: U.S. Government Printing Office, November 8, 1985), Serial No. 99-41, p. 20.

[31] Westat, Inc., *An Overview of JTPA PY84 Title III Activities in Fifty States* (Rockville, Maryland: Westat, Inc., May 8, 1985), p. 9.

[32] William Gainer, U.S. General Accounting Office, in U.S. Congress, House Committee on Education and Labor, Subcommittee on Employment Opportunities, *Oversight Hearing on the Job Training Partnership Act (Part 3)* (Washington: U.S. Government Printing Office, November 8, 1985), Serial No. 99-41, pp. 12, 23.

[33] U.S. General Accounting Office, *Dislocated Workers: Extent of Business Closures, Layoffs, and the Public and Private Response* (Washington: GAO, July 1986), HRD-86-116BR, p. 36.

34 U.S. Office of Technology Assessment, *Technology and Structural Unemployment: Reemploying Displaced Adults* (Washington: U.S. Government Printing Office, February 1986), OTA-ITE-250, p. 176.

35 Francis W. Horvath, "The Pulse of Economic Change: Displaced Workers of 1981-85," *Monthly Labor Review,* June 1987, p. 7.

36 U.S. Office of Technology Assessment, *Plant Closing: Advance Notice and Rapid Response* (Washington: Government Printing Office, September 1986), OTA-ITE-321, pp. 1, 21-2.

37 Secretary of Labor's Task Force on Economic Adjustment and Worker Dislocation, *Economic Adjustment and Worker Dislocation in a Competitive Society,* U.S. Department of Labor, December 1986, p. 22.

38 Robert Cook (ed.), *Worker Dislocation* (Kalamazoo, Michigan: W.E. Upjohn Institute for Employment Research, 1987).

6. The Job Corps: Investing Pays Off

1 Human Environment Center, *Conservation and Service Corps Profiles* (Washington: Human Environment Center, November 1986), pp. 1-5; Public/Private Ventures, *The California Conservation Corps* (Philadelphia: Public/Private Ventures, June 1987) and *Youth Corps Profiles* (Philadelphia: Public/Private Ventures, December 1986).

2 Abt Associates, Inc., *An Assessment of Funding Allocation Under the Job Training Partnership Act* (Cambridge, Massachusetts: Abt Associates, Inc., August 31, 1986), p. 103.

3 Office of Job Corps, *Vocational Education Offerings Review: Documentation Report No. 1* (Washington: U.S. Department of Labor, September 1983), p 10.

4 U.S. House of Representatives, *Congressional Record,* March 5, 1985, p. H 1029.

5 Peter Rell, Job Corps director, in U.S. Congress, House Committee on Education and Labor, Subcommittee on Employment Opportunities, *Job Corps Center Closings and Slot Reductions* (Washington: U.S. Government Printing Office, May 15, 1986), Serial No. 99-116, p. 55.

6 Representatives from RCA, Singer and Teledyne, in U.S. Congress, House Committee on Government Operations, Manpower and Housing Subcommittee, *Administration of the Job Corps Program by the Employment and Training Administration of the Department of Labor* (Washington: U.S. Government Printing Office, September 26, 1984), pp. 4-5, 45.

[7] Memorandum from Roberts T. Jones, Office of Job Training Programs, August 1, 1984, in U.S. Congress, House Committee on Government Operations, Employment and Housing Subcommittee, *The Job Corps: Do Its Benefits Outweigh the Costs?* (Washington: U.S. Government Printing Office, May 23, 1985), pp. 11-14.

[8] Robert Taggart, *A Fisherman's Guide* (Kalamazoo, Michigan: W.E. Upjohn Institute for Employment Research, 1981), p. 49.

[9] Macro Systems, Inc., *Job Corps Process Analysis: Final Report* (Silver Spring, Maryland: Macro Systems, Inc., October 1985), p. 11:3, Exhibit 11:2.

[10] U.S. General Accounting Office, *Job Corps* (Washington: GAO, July 1986), HRD-86-121BR, pp. 7-9, 11, 14; Office of Job Corps, *Vocational Education Offerings Review: Documentation Report No. 4* (Washington: U.S. Department of Labor, September 1983), p. 7.

[11] U.S. General Accounting Office, *Job Corps Should Strengthen Eligibility Requirements and Fully Disclose Performance* (Washington: GAO, July 9, 1979), HRD-79-60, pp. 1, 13.

[12] U.S. Department of Labor, *Semiannual Report of the Inspector General, October 1, 1984-March 31, 1985* (Washington: U.S. Department of Labor, 1985), pp. 12-13; Macro Systems, Inc., *Job Corps Process Analysis: Final Report* (Silver Spring, Maryland: Macro Systems, Inc., October 1985), pp. 3:12-23.

[13] Office of Job Corps, *Vocational Educational Offerings Review: Documentation Report No. 1* (Washington: U.S. Department of Labor, September 1983), p. 16.

[14] Except where other sources are cited, this section is based on Macro Systems, Inc., *Job Corps Process Analysis: Final Report* (Silver Spring, Maryland: Macro Systems, Inc., October 1985), Chapter 4.

[15] Phone conversation with John Amos, Office of Job Corps, July 26, 1987; Macro Systems, Inc., *Job Corps Process Analysis: Final Report* (Silver Spring, Maryland: Macro Systems, Inc., October 1985) p. 4:23.

[16] Mathematica Policy Research, Inc., *Evaluation of the Economic Impact of the Job Corps Program: Third Follow-Up Report* (Princeton, New Jersey: Mathematica Policy Research, Inc., September 1982), p. 123.

[17] Robert Taggart, *A Fisherman's Guide* (Kalamazoo, Michigan: W.E. Upjohn Institute for Employment Research, 1981), p. 125.

[18] Macro Systems, Inc., *Job Corps Process Analysis: Final Report (Silver Spring, Maryland: Macro Systems, Inc., October 1985)*, pp. 5:9-11, 20-5.

[19] Office of Job Corps, *Job Corps Vocational Offerings Review: Final Report* (Washington: U.S. Department of Labor, October 1983), pp. 21-4, 26-7; Macro Systems, Inc., *Job Corps Process Analysis: Final Report* (Silver Spring, Maryland: Macro Systems, Inc., October 1985), pp. 5:12-14, 28-30.

[20] Macro Systems, Inc., *Job Corps Process Analysis: Final Report* (Silver Spring, Maryland: Macro Systems, Inc., October 1985), pp. 5:5-6, 19-20, 26-8, 31.

[21] This section is based on Macro Systems, Inc., *Job Corps Process Analysis: Final Report* (Silver Spring, Maryland: Macro Systems, Inc., October 1985), Chapters 6-8.

[22] Patricia Auspos and Marilyn Price, *Launching Jobstart* (New York: Manpower Demonstration Research Corporation, January 1987).

[23] U.S. Department of Labor, Employment and Training Administration, *Review of Selected Aspects of the Job Corps Program,* July 1982, pp. 41, 44.

[24] Macro System, Inc., *Job Corps Process Analysis: Final Report* (Silver Spring, Maryland: Macro Systems, Inc., October 1985), pp. 9:3, 7-16.

[25] Macro Systems, Inc., *Jobs Corps Process Analysis: Final Report* (Silver Spring, Maryland: Macro Systems, Inc., October 1985), pp. 3:26-9, 30-2, 7:6-7, 9:5-7; U.S. Department of Labor, Employment and Training Administration, *Review of Selected Aspects of the Job Corps Program,* July 1982, p. 42.

[26] Rodriguez, Roach & Associates, P.C., *Special Review of Screening and Placement* (Washington: U.S. Department of Labor, August 12, 1983), pp. 21, 47-8.

[27] Robert Taggart, *A Fisherman's Guide* (Kalamazoo, Michigan: W.E. Upjohn Institute for Employment Research, 1981), p. 268.

[28] Mathematica Policy Research, Inc., *Evaluation of the Economic Impact of the Job Corps Program: Third Follow-up Report* (Princeton, New Jersey: Mathematica Policy Research, Inc., September 1982), pp. 111, 118, 121, 130-1, 157, 177-9.

[29] Mathematica Policy Research, Inc., *Relative Effectiveness of Job Corps Vocational Training by Occupational Groupings* (Princeton, New Jersey: Mathematica Policy Research, Inc., March 1983), pp. 8-12.

[30] Mathematica Policy Research, Inc., *Evaluation of the Economic Impact of the Job Corps Program: Third Follow-up Report* (Princeton, New Jersey: Mathematica Policy Research, Inc., September 1982), pp. 241, 248, 251, 253.

7. Farmworker and Indian Programs

[1] Cited in Edward F. Dement, *Out of Sight, Out of Mind* (Washington: National Governors' Association, August 1985) p. 4.

[2] Philip L. Martin, *Seasonal Workers in American Agriculture* (Washington: National Commission for Employment Policy, March 1985), RR-85-04, pp. 8-9; Edward F. Dement, *Out of Sight, Out of Mind* (Washington: National Governors' Association, August 1985), p. 14.

[3] Sorensen & Brough, *Special Purpose Reviews of DOL Migrant and Seasonal Farmworkers Programs* (Washington: U.S. Department of Labor, January 23, 1986), pp. 7, 22; U.S. Department of Labor, *Semiannual Report of the Inspector General, October 31, 1985-March 31, 1986* and *April 1, 1986-September 30, 1986* (Washington: U.S. Department of Labor, 1986), Appendix tables.

[4] Sorensen & Brough, *Special Purpose Reviews of DOL Migrant and Seasonal Farmworkers Programs* (Washington: U.S. Department of Labor, January 23, 1986), pp. 15-16, 29, and *Program Results Review* (Washington: U.S. Department of Labor, 1986), pp. 18-19.

[5] Sorensen & Brough, *Special Purpose Reviews of DOL Migrant and Seasonal Farmworkers Programs* (Washington: U.S. Department of Labor, January 23, 1986), pp. 13-14.

[6] Lawrence Johnson & Associates, Inc., *Evaluation of Selected Aspects of the Migrant and Seasonal Farmworker Program* (Washington: Lawrence Johnson & Associates, Inc., April 11, 1985) pp. x, 4:23, 6:2.

[7] Lawrence Johnson & Associates, Inc., *Evaluation of Selected Aspects of the Migrant and Seasonal Farmworkers Program* (Washington: Lawrence Johnson & Associates, Inc., April 11, 1985), pp. 4:22, 5:1, 8; Sorensen & Brough, Program Results Review (Washington: U.S. Department of Labor, 1986), pp. 17-21.

[8] Sar A. Levitan, *Programs in Aid of the Poor* (Baltimore, Maryland: The Johns Hopkins University Press, 1985), p. 132.

[9] Bureau of Indian Affairs, *Indian Service Population and Labor Force Estimates* (Washington: U.S. Department of the Interior, January 1987), p. 3.

[10] U.S. Department of Labor, *Semiannual Report of the Inspector General,* various years (Washington: U.S. Department of Labor, 1984-7), Appendix tables.

[11] Polaris Research and Development, *The Indian and Native American Employment and Training Program* (San Francisco: Polaris Research and Development, January 1985), pp. 4:22-6, 5:24, 31-2, 42, 44, 47-8, 53-4, 6:17 (draft).

[12] Indian and Native American Employment and Training Coalition, "The DOL/SRI 'Model' for Setting Performance Standards for Indian and Native American JTPA Programs," October 13, 1986, pp. 7-8 (mimeo).

[13] Polaris Research and Development, *The Indian and Native American Employment and Training Program* (San Francisco: Polaris Research and Development, January 1985), pp. 3:43-50 (draft).

8. Taking Stock

[1] Robert Taggart, "A Business Approach to Social Programming," prepared for the Ford Foundation Social Welfare Policy Project, September 1986.

[2] James L. Sundquist, "Has America Lost Its Social Conscience — And How Will It Get It Back?," *Political Science Quarterly*, Issue No. 4, 1986, p. 521.

Index

211

212